# Write! Science
## Multiple Intelligences & Cooperative Learning Writing Activities

### Virginia DeBolt

©1998 by *Kagan Cooperative Learning*

This book is published by *Kagan Cooperative Learning*. All rights are reserved by *Kagan Cooperative Learning*. No part of this publication may be reproduced or transmitted in any form by any means, electronic or mechanical, including photocopy, recording, or any information storage and retrieval system, without prior written permission from *Kagan Cooperative Learning*. The blackline masters included in this book are intended for duplication only by classroom teachers who purchase the book, for use limited to their own classrooms. To obtain additional copies of this book, or information regarding workshops in cooperative learning, contact:

*Kagan Cooperative Learning*
1160 Calle Cordillera
San Clemente, CA 92673
**1(800) WEE CO-OP**
www.KaganCoopLearn.com

ISBN: 1-879097-39-7

# Table of Contents

*Chart of Structures ... III*
*Acknowledgements ... IV*

## Part I — Integrating Writing and Science ...... 1

10 Rules for Writers .................... 14
The Writing Process.................... 15
Proofreader's Marks.................... 16
Peer Conference Gambit Cards........... 17
Peer Conference Response Form ......... 18
Peer Response (Rough Draft) ........... 19

## Part II — Science Writing Activities ........... 21

1  I Want to Know ................... 22
2  Industry and the Environment ....... 24
3  Evaluate the Alternatives ........... 28
4  Prioritize the Problems ............. 33
5  Propose the Solution ............... 36
6  I Believe... ....................... 40
7  A New Invention ................... 42
8  Evaluate a Product ................ 44
9  Create a Question.................. 46
10 Internet Research ................. 48
11 Classify This!..................... 50
12 Compare and Contrast ............. 52
13 The Advantages and Disadvantages ... 54
14 Chart the Steps ................... 56
15 A Scientific Breakthrough .......... 60
16 Graphic Conclusions ............... 62
17 Science News Report .............. 64
18 Science Log ....................... 66

19 Interviews About You................ 68
20 Define This! ....................... 70
21 Science Books..................... 72
22 Science or Fiction? ................. 76
23 How Does This Thing Work? ......... 78
24 Concept Mobile .................... 80
25 Make A Myth ...................... 82
26 Animal Adaptations ................ 84
27 Outline Review..................... 86
28 Science Jeopardy................... 88
29 What I Learned.................... 90
30 Some Interesting Consequences ....... 92
31 Experiment Reflections ............. 96
32 Singing Science.................... 98
33 Creature Creation.................. 100
34 Analyze Cause and Effect........... 102
35 My Opinion ....................... 104
36 Why It's Important................. 108

Virginia DeBolt: *Write! Science*
Kagan Cooperative Learning • 1 (800) WEE CO-OP

# Table of Contents

## Part III — Cooperative Learning Structures .... 111

1. Agreement Circles ................. 112
2. Corners ......................... 113
3. 4S Brainstorming ................. 114
4. Mix-Freeze-Pair .................. 114
5. Pair Discussion .................. 115
6. Pair Project .................... 115
7. Pairs Check ..................... 116
8. Pairs Present ................... 117
9. RallyTable ...................... 117
10. RoundRobin ..................... 118
11. RoundTable ..................... 118
12. Send-A-Problem ................. 119
13. Simultaneous Chalkboard Share ... 120
14. Simultaneous RoundTable ........ 120
15. Team Discussion ................ 121
16. Team Interview ................. 121
17. Team Project ................... 122
18. Team Sort ...................... 123
19. Teams Present .................. 124
20. Team Word Web .................. 125
21. ThinkPad Brainstorming ......... 126
22. Think-Pair-Share ............... 127
23. Think-Pair-Write ............... 128
24. Think-Write-Pair-Share ......... 129
25. Think-Write-RoundRobin ......... 130
26. Unstructured Sort .............. 131
27. Write-Pair-Share ............... 132

*Bibliography* ...133
*About the Author* ...134

### Journal Topic Chart

You will find Journal Topics on pages:

**27, 31, 35, 39, 59, 75, 95, 107**

# Chart of Structures

| Structure | Basic Description | See Also Activities |
|---|---|---|
| Agreement Circles | 112 | 35 |
| Corners | 113 | 26 |
| 4S Brainstorming | 114 | 2, 19 |
| Mix-Freeze-Pair | 114 | 36 |
| Pair Discussion | 115 | 26 |
| Pair Project | 115 | 12, 14, 22, 30, 32, 34 |
| Pairs Check | 116 | 20 |
| Pairs Present | 117 | 22, 32, 34 |
| RallyTable | 117 | 29 |
| RoundRobin | 118 | 3, 6, 8, 10, 13, 14, 16, 17, 19, 21, 23, 25, 26, 28, 29, 30, 33, 35 |
| RoundTable | 118 | 3, 27 |
| Send-A-Problem | 119 | 9 |
| Simultaneous Chalkboard Share | 120 | 11, 32 |
| Simultaneous RoundTable | 120 | 19, 21 |
| Team Discussion | 121 | 13, 21 |
| Team Interview | 121 | 7, 15 |
| Team Project | 122 | 10, 21, 24 |
| Team Sort | 123 | 4 |
| Teams Present | 124 | 21, 24 |
| Team Word Web | 125 | 5 |
| ThinkPad Brainstorming | 126 | 3, 4, 13 |
| Think-Pair-Share | 127 | 6, 30 |
| Think-Pair-Write | 128 | 31 |
| Think-Write-Pair-Share | 129 | 1, 17 |
| Think-Write-RoundRobin | 130 | 5, 25 |
| Unstructured Sort | 131 | 11 |
| Write-Pair-Share | 132 | 18 |

Virginia DeBolt: *Write! Science*
Kagan Cooperative Learning • 1 (800) WEE CO-OP

# Acknowledgements

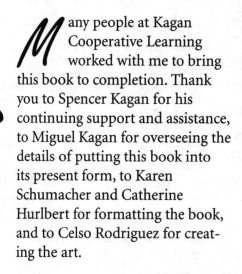

Many people at Kagan Cooperative Learning worked with me to bring this book to completion. Thank you to Spencer Kagan for his continuing support and assistance, to Miguel Kagan for overseeing the details of putting this book into its present form, to Karen Schumacher and Catherine Hurlbert for formatting the book, and to Celso Rodriguez for creating the art.

My scientific teammate at Murchison Middle School, Karen Green, gave me the interview ideas for Activity 19, as well as ongoing support and science-minded ideas.

# Part I

# Integrating Writing and Science

*"Countless careers rise or fall on the ability or inability of employees to state a set of facts, summarize a meeting or present an idea coherently."*

–William Zinsser

Today's teachers are encouraged to include writing in all the subject areas, including science. Writing during science or in the science classroom may feel foreign at first. Numbers and symbols are perceived to be the language of science. However, integrating writing in science enhances and improves students' understanding of science. Writing is a tool for learning in science as surely as a dissection kit or a beaker. Teachers can use writing as part of daily instruction. Students can use writing in science, not as a novelist or poet would use writing, but the way a scientist would use writing.

To write is to compose. To compose well is to comprehend. Writing is not speaking, where we hope that the, ahh, listeners, like, you know, get it. Writing demands careful word choice, clear thinking, complete communication. The physical act of writing takes longer than thinking or speaking, and so seems to allow the brain time for the discoveries and connections writers often make while writing. Professional writers, when asked to explain why they write, often answer that they write to find out what they're thinking, what they know and what it means. As students write, they develop their knowledge of a subject. They discover, organize, classify, connect and evaluate information.

Integrating writing and science moves students beyond the basic facts of science. Writing allows students to look critically and creatively at science, enriching students' understanding and

| <u>Writing to Learn</u> | vs. | <u>Reading to Learn</u> |
|---|---|---|
| What do you have to say? | | What did they have to say? |
| Be active. Do it. | | Sit still. Pay attention. |
| Student chooses the words. | | Teacher chooses the words. |
| Productive. Output. | | Consumptive. Input. |

Virginia DeBolt: *Write! Science*
Kagan Cooperative Learning • 1 (800) WEE CO-OP

appreciation of science. By writing about science, students are doing the work of true scientist; learning becomes more real and more meaningful. As you integrate writing and science, think of it as an enhancement to teaching science rather than as one more thing to cram into an already crowded curriculum.

Indeed, writing is a terrific tool for teaching science as well as the other disciplines, but it is more than that. Writing is a life skill, highly valued by society. Writing is everywhere. Every aspect of human endeavor needs writing about—how else would we pass along the information? The box below is a partial list of things people write or write about. Notice how diverse the writings are.

This list is not at all complete. Wander through the nonfiction stacks in your library. People write about everything. Most writing today is nonfiction, and the need for nonfiction writers continues to grow. Expanding technology in an information age demands it. Nonfiction has never been so important. We are building our national future on information and writers are in demand to explain it. We live in a wired world where communication is essential. Writing across the curriculum gives students the ability to think and communicate today and tomorrow.

## So, What Do I Need to Know About Writing?

Enough about the rationale for integrating writing. You're probably reading this book now because you're already convinced about the value of writing. So what do you need to know? The first thing you and your students should know about writing is that there are 10 rules to writing that

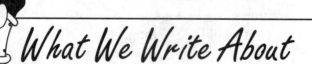

### What We Write About

- advertisements
- agendas
- animal medicine
- animals
- annotated calendars
- art
- autobiographies
- awards and inscriptions
- biographies
- biology
- business
- captions and labels
- cartoons
- case studies
- chemistry
- coin new words
- collecting
- computer programs
- concerts
- constellations
- contest entries
- dance
- diaries and journals
- drug abuse
- e mail
- economics
- editorials and opinions
- essays
- eulogies
- fashion
- features
- field guides
- field journals
- film
- folk remedies
- folk traditions
- folklore
- foreign language journaling
- forms
- games and puzzles
- geography
- history

Virginia DeBolt: *Write! Science*

# Integrating Writing and Science

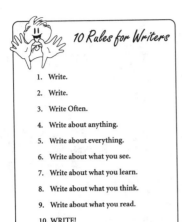

**10 Rules for Writers**

1. Write.
2. Write.
3. Write Often.
4. Write about anything.
5. Write about everything.
6. Write about what you see.
7. Write about what you learn.
8. Write about what you think.
9. Write about what you read.
10. WRITE!

**The Writing Process**

are absolutely critical. See the 10 Rules at left. These 10 rules are a way to emphasize that the road to becoming a better writer (and scientist) is to write, write, and write some more! Use these 10 rules as a handout or overhead as you describe the use of writing to your students (see page 14).

The next thing about writing you and your students should know is that writing is considered a process—the Writing Process. This process includes prewriting, revising, editing, proofreading and publishing. Publishing is not necessarily a "publication." Publishing could be reading work aloud to the class, posting work on a bulletin board, polishing an essay to turn in to the teacher or other types of sharing. Teaching students to move about in the process of writing is often considered as important as the final written product.

The writing process is not linear. It is a circular process. At any point, students can confer, evaluate, and rewrite. For that reason, the writing process is put in a wheel with Conferring/Evaluating/Rewriting in the center of the wheel (see page 15).

The activities in this book focus heavily on the prewriting and writing stages of the process. We've already covered writing, what's so important about prewriting? It's the time when concepts form, vocabulary develops, ideas grow from the synergy of interaction with other students. Prewriting is a social act. Students talk, banter, give and receive feedback. Prewriting develops the readiness to write. Prewriting primes the pump from which the writing will pour.

In the activities in this book, students discuss, plan, outline and brainstorm cooperatively before

## What We Write About

- humor
- instructions and advice
- interactive media
- interviews
- learning logs
- lists and notes
- literature
- medicine
- memoirs
- memoranda and messages
- mottoes and slogans
- music
- mythology
- nature

- news stories
- office business
- oral histories
- parodies
- petitions
- philosophy
- physics
- public notices
- recipes
- reports of current events
- research reports
- resumes and cover letters
- reviews
- rules and regulations

- scrapbooks
- simulations
- song lyrics
- sports
- technology
- telegrams
- textbooks
- thumbnail sketches
- time capsule lists
- travel

Virginia DeBolt: *Write! Science*
Kagan Cooperative Learning • 1 (800) WEE CO-OP

they actually do any writing. The reason is because prewriting makes writing easier and better. Writers will tell you that they are always writing. A composition of words swirls inside the brain no matter what else a writer might appear to be doing. When a writer sits down to write, it may seem that the words flow easily, when actually considerable time was spent on the words already.

Since most students will not be rehearsing compositions during their spare moments, you can improve the quality of what students write by providing ample time for prewriting activities. As a rule of thumb, the more time you allow for prewriting, the better the writing will be. Therefore, if you draw from only one aspect of the writing process, let it be prewriting.

But prewriting and writing are not the whole story for integrating writing and science. Consider these examples: *Lives of a Cell* by Lewis Thomas, *Silent Spring* by Rachel Carson, *Voyage of the Beagle* by Charles Darwin, *The Immense Journey* by Loren Eisley. These books contain some of the most powerful and beautiful language ever written. Like all good writing, these books were not just written. They were revised, proofread, carefully edited, and finally published, to be shared with others.

Sharing and publishing are extremely important parts of the writing process, not to be overlooked. By sharing, students can learn from each other what good writing looks and sounds like. Since the writing is about science, students become their own science teachers as they share their learning, connections and reflections.

Many activities include a sharing component. You can easily have students read any of their writing to a partner, to teammates, or even to the entire class. Students can also share their writing by exchanging papers or by posting their papers in a location where classmates can read them. Sharing and publishing make writing a learning experience not only for the writer, but for the recipient as well.

## Peer Editing and Conferencing

The science writing activities in this book focus primarily on using writing as a means to teach science. The emphasis is more on the content than the writing itself. However, with a little work, any writing assignment can be easily turned into a polished work of art. What do you do when students need to revise, proofread and edit? Let students help each other. Establish small groups for peer editing and conferencing.

Students offer each other valuable ideas about writing. Since students identify with the words they write and can be

Virginia DeBolt: *Write! Science*

# Integrating Writing and Science

eternally wounded by thoughtless critical comments, your task is to keep the conferences positive. Because students can sometimes be masters of the outspoken insult, it helps to establish a few basic rules for peer conferences, such as:

- Begin with positive comments about what is good in the writing.
- Ask questions that help the writer discover ways to change writing for the better, like:

  "I don't understand, could you explain this part a little more?"

  "Do you think it would help to change the order of these paragraphs?"

  "Would you like for me to underline the words I think you've spelled wrong?"

- Remember that the writer is the final judge of how the writing should be changed

As a peer conference technique, teaching students to ask questions about another's writing works well. The questions become an indicator of where the writing needs to be changed and improved. There are fewer hurt feelings and arguments because the writers learn what doesn't work in their writing without hearing comments such as, "That third paragraph really stinks—throw it out."

It will help students maintain a positive attitude toward each other if you brainstorm with them to develop a list of ways to say things that help without hurt or insult. Ask them, "How would you like to be told that your writing was disorganized or unclear?" Post their ideas for easy viewing.

In the back of this chapter, you will find a number of forms that will be helpful for peer editing and conferencing. On page 16, there is a Proofreader's Marks form. Have students use these standard marks as they edit each other's papers. For consistency, use them yourself as you edit students' papers.

On page 17 there are gambit cards for students to use in peer conferences. These gambit cards are sentence starters for students as they have peer conferences. They direct the conference and promote a positive tone.

The Peer Conference Response Form is another form helpful for peer conferences, see page 18. Have students fill out their response form before the peer conference, then students go over their comments together.

Page 19 is a Peer Response Form. Students write in the lined space provided. When done, they give it to a peer to respond to the writing in the left margin. They then meet to go over the responses.

## What About Grading?

A writing assignment will sink into quicksand if students think they won't be graded. The type of grading you do largely depends on

Virginia DeBolt: *Write! Science*
Kagan Cooperative Learning • 1 (800) WEE CO-OP

the type and frequency of writing assignments students do. I suggest an on-going, long-term approach to writing and grading, using writing journals and a writing portfolio. We will look at both journals and portfolios in depth after some general comments on grading.

The first comment on grading is: Don't make grading too labor-intensive for yourself to limit the frequency and volume of student writing. The more students write, the more they learn. More writing also means more grading and more work for you, right? Not necessarily. If you have unlimited time and energy, grade and respond to every writing assignment. If not, grade everything but don't read everything. Yes, grade everything but don't read everything. Students need to know that everything they write might be read, but that doesn't mean you have to read everything. We'll examine this idea in more detail in the sections on journals and portfolios.

The second general comment on grading is: Align your grading practices with the type of writing students do. Glance through the journal topics and activities in this book. You will see a range of writing assignments. You should use a different grading approach depending on the type of writing.

Writing assignments that check for understanding should be turned in for immediate response while the topic is still fresh. Elaborate writing assignments like reports and final papers require individual attention, feedback and usually impact a student's course grade. With most other activities and journal writings, the process of writing and sharing is more important than the evaluation. Students can save these assignments for periodic journal and portfolio checks.

A multipronged approach to grading allows the teacher to hold students accountable for even the most frequent writing assignments, yet at the same time, makes it unnecessary for the teacher to read every word the student writes.

## Writing Journals

Some writing might be done in a daily journal. A spiral-bound notebook is a nice way to keep all journal writing assignments together.

Good journal topics are reusable.
- Write for five minutes about yesterday's homework.
- Tell everything you learned about _____ today.
- What did you miss on the test? Do you know it now?
- Summarize last night's reading assignment.
- We are beginning a new chapter. Write everything you already know about it. Tell what you want to know about it.

## Integrating Writing and Science

- Write about the hardest or most confusing part of _____.

Journals can be easily individualized. Students who benefit from the use of clusters and mind maps might use the left pages for that and the right pages for writing. Students who learn or remember with pictures and symbols can incorporate visuals in their journal. Quotes from the text might be written on one side of a page, and the student's response to the quotes on the other. Journal writing is private, although it may be shared with classmates and will be shared with the teacher. Nevertheless, it is a student's personal record of growth, progress, learning, and individual revelations about personal learning styles and successes.

**Journal Topics**

You will find Journal Topics on pages:

27, 31, 35, 39, 59, 75, 95, 107

You will find Journal Topics scattered throughout the activities section of this book. For quick reference, see the Journal Topics chart at left.

A check, check minus or check plus may be used to check for the quality of writing. If you don't have the time to read all journals, use a plus or minus in your grade book to indicate whether or not a student has completed each journal assignment. To keep up with journals on a daily basis, I suggest that in each period you collect, read and respond to three journals In ten days, (two weeks) you will have read thirty students' journals. Read only the journal entry from the day you collect the journal, but do a quick flip-through to be sure the student is writing all the assignments. Reading and responding to three journal entries a day should take no more than five minutes. Journals can be returned to the students or to a storage area immediately.

To respond to a journal entry, simply read it and write a quick response. The teacher is rather like a pen pal, exchanging ideas informally with the writer. What sort of response do you make to a journal entry? Ask a question designed to make the student dig deeper. Give a helpful comment that might clear up a problem. Give praise for good thinking. Focus on the academic subject under consideration. One good question or comment is enough. What your response really does is tell the student that his or her learning process is important to you, that you consider it worth recording and reflecting upon, and that the student is a major participant in his or her own learning.

## Writing Portfolio

Have students keep their writing activities from this book in a three ring binder. This collection of writing activities serves as a writing portfolio. Students need to know that writing they do will be graded somehow, even if it's just for completeness, and that you have a serious commitment to that part of your curriculum. You can grade the material in the binder periodically, perhaps every six weeks.

A more differentiated approach to grading portfolios may include developing a workable grading matrix based on requirements such as completeness, organization, appearance, or other criteria you consider important. You may ask students to provide a table of contents, index, tabs and other helpful aids in their binder. The writing portfolio becomes a record of what the students have learned as well as how students' writing has developed over time. In addition to using the portfolio for grading, have students use it as a tool for reflection about their progress in writing and learning in science.

## Using the Writing Activities

In this book you'll find a variety of types of writing activities like: Writing that enables the student to reflect on his or her thinking; writing that enables the student to remember, clarify, and connect new learning to previous knowledge; writing that augments classroom discussions and activities; writing that lets the teacher see into the student's thought processes; and writing that demonstrates learning to a specified audience.

Many of the writing activities in this book are general, and intentionally so. Because curriculum varies from grade-to-grade and class-to-class, these activities were designed as close to "one size fits all" as possible.

For specific content applications of the activity, see the Idea Bank in each activity for a number of ideas. There is also space under More Ideas for My Class for you to fill in ideas to use the activity with your own curriculum. As you read the activity, make sure to fill in additional ideas. That way, when you begin a topic or unit you can flip through the activities to find the ones that will apply.

Many of the activities can be used meaningfully more than once with new content. Some you may find yourself returning to time and time again.

Between the activities, the journal topics, the ideas for my class, and your own writing ideas, you should have more than enough writing topics and activities to integrate writing into your science curriculum all year long.

The writing activities you'll find in this book were designed to incorporate three progressive movements in education: cooperative learning, multiple intelligences, and higher-level thinking. Let's take a quick look at each innovation and how each are included in these activities. We will briefly examine Spencer Kagan's

# Integrating Writing and Science

**Kagan's 6 Key Concepts**

1. Teams
2. Will
3. Management
4. Skills
5. Basic Principles
6. Structures

approach to cooperative learning, Howard Gardner's theory of multiple intelligences, and Benjamin Bloom's taxonomy of thinking.

## Cooperative Learning

Research has found that cooperative learning promotes higher achievement than competitive and individualistic learning structures across all age levels, subject areas, and almost all tasks. Writing and science are no exceptions!

Cooperative learning is a natural partner of writing. Cooperative work provides a place for students to brainstorm ideas, develop language and vocabulary, get constructive feedback, and share final works.

Small group interaction provides students with a less threatening environment in which to share their writing and gives every student an equal opportunity to be an active participant throughout the stages of the writing process. An at-risk student, who may have given up on class participation in a whole class structure, is "hooked in" to small group processes and becomes a contributor rather than a distracter.

Cooperative groups supply the teacher with a positive method of channeling the energy to socialize and interact into productive work.

The activities in this book focus on Dr. Spencer Kagan's approach to cooperative learning. For more details on the theory, research and application of cooperative learning, see Dr. Kagan's popular and comprehensive book, *Cooperative Learning*, available from Kagan Cooperative Learning.

In his book, Dr. Kagan outlines six key concepts helpful for making cooperative learning a success in the class. (See box at left.) Many of these key concepts are integrated into the activities in this book, especially the cooperative learning structures. The activities in this book work well as stand-alone cooperative events, but work even better in a cooperative classroom environment. Kagan's six keys to cooperative learning are as follows:

### 1. Teams

A team is a small group of students who work together. For these activities, teams of four are ideal. They are small enough for active participation and split evenly for equal participation during pair work. Teams should be carefully selected by the teacher to reflect a mixture of ability levels, gender and ethnicity. Teams should stay together for approximately six weeks.

### 2. Will

For cooperative learning to run successfully, students must have the will to cooperate. Classbuilding and teambuilding activities give students the opportunity to interact with teammates and classmates in a positive way, promote an environment conducive to successful teamwork, and create a positive class atmosphere. There are three great activity books available from Kagan Cooperative Learning that I can recommend to create the "Will" to cooperate: *Classbuilding, Teambuilding,* and *Communitybuilding.*

### 3. Management
A number of cooperative management tools helps the teacher run the cooperative classroom more effectively. Kagan describes a host of management tools including using a quiet signal, assigning roles, using modeling, team questions, and more.

### 4. Skills
Students need social skills such as listening, conflict resolution, and tutoring to work together successfully. Social skills can be taught directly, but with some direction, many can be naturally acquired in the context of cooperative learning.

### 5. Basic Principles
The are four basic principles to successful cooperative learning summarized by the acronym PIES: **P**ositive Interdependence, **I**ndividual Accountability, **E**qual Participation and **S**imultaneous Interaction. The box at right illustrates the four basic principles and the critical question associated with each principle.

 **Positive Interdependence**
Kagan defines positive interdependence as, "Two individuals are mutually positively interdependent if the gains of either helps the other…Strong Positive Interdependence is created when a student cannot make a gain without a gain of another student. Weak Positive Interdependence is created when a gain for one may produce a gain for another, but it is not *necessary* (italics added)." Students are positively interdependent as they work together to help each other with their writing and learning.

 **Individual Accountability**
Individual Accountability means that each student is responsible for, and graded on, his or her own learning, contribution, and performance. A student might be held accountable for helping another student learn a new skill in a Pairs Check activity. A student might be held accountable for listening in a Paraphrase activity. A student might be held accountable for learning by passing a test. Most activities have an independent writing component that can be used to hold students accountable for sharing or turning in.

 **Equal Participation**
Equal Participation means that each student has an equal chance to speak, to read, to offer answers and to think. Guarantee Equal Participation by structuring activities so that

## PIES
### The Principles of Cooperative Learning

*Is a gain for one, a gain for another? Is help necessary?*

*Is individual public performance required?*

*How equal is the participation?*

*What percent are overtly active at once?*

Virginia DeBolt: *Write! Science*

everyone must participate. Assigning roles is one way to accomplish this. If each person has a job to do, each person is participating. Equal Participation can also be created by using turn taking and turn-taking structures. Turn-taking structures include RoundRobin, RoundTable, RallyRobin, RallyTable, Think-Pair-Share, Three-Step Interview and Pairs Check.

### Simultaneous Interaction

Simultaneous Interaction gives you and your students the gift of time. Time for students to read their writing aloud. Time for language development during prewriting. Time for students to manage their own revising and editing when necessary.

How does Simultaneous Interaction give you time? Suppose, for example, that the students have written about the most difficult aspect of their last homework assignment. Having each student share with the class for one minute would take over half an hour. Instead, by pairing students to interact simultaneously to read aloud and discuss their writing, everyone in class can share and respond to the homework in a couple of minutes. In addition to the benefit gained from writing about the homework, students have received the further benefit of speaking and being listened to about it. The time effect of Simultaneous Interaction applies to any writing activity from prewriting to publishing.

Incorporating these four principles in your class activities will insure that you have real, successful cooperative learning happening in your room as opposed to simple group work. These principles are "built-into" the cooperative strategies used throughout the activities.

### 6. Structures

Structures like RoundRobin and Think-Pair-Share are simple cooperative strategies teachers to use to create learning activities. Structures describe how students interact over the content. There are many structures, each designed to reach different educational objectives.

The activities in this book are based on cooperative structures. Many activities include one cooperative structure, and independent writing. Some activities lead students through a number of cooperative strategies. The procedure for using each cooperative structure is described in each activity. The cooperative structure is listed in the Cooperative Learning section of the intro page. A glossary of structures is provided in the back of the book for easy reference.

## Multiple Intelligences

The basic premise of multiple intelligences is that people are smart in many ways. Some people are particularly good with words; some people are good with math and logic; some people are especially talented with art and spatial relations; some people are good with their hands and bodies; some people are good with music and rhythm; some people are in tune with others; some people are in tune with themselves; and some people are in tune with nature.

Howard Gardner, the originator or the theory of multiple intelligences, called each one of these ways of being smart an intelligence. He originally identified seven intelligences and has added the eighth, the Naturalist. Gardner's eight intelligences are as follows (see box at right):

1. **Verbal/Linguistic**
2. **Logical/Mathematical**
3. **Visual/Spatial**
4. **Bodily/Kinesthetic**
5. **Musical/Rhythmic**
6. **Interpersonal**
7. **Intrapersonal**
8. **Naturalist**

The implication of the multiple intelligences theory for the classroom is that since students are so diverse, classroom learning should reflect the range of intelligences. Students should be given opportunities to develop their strengths as well as opportunities to develop their weaknesses. See the box below for activities ideas for the multiple intelligences.

Integrating writing and science takes naturalist and logical/mathematical content and translates it into a verbal/linguistic form. Teachers can more easily reach and teach linguistic learners. But the activities in this book are much more than solitary writing

### The 8 Intelligences

- Verbal/Linguistic
- Logical/Mathematical
- Visual/Spatial
- Bodily/Kinesthetic
- Musical/Rhythmic
- Interpersonal
- Intrapersonal
- Naturalist

## Activities for the Multiple Intelligences

Here is a brief list of activities to consider to activate the multiple intelligences.

**Verbal/Linguistic**
essay, journal, debate, storytelling, portfolios

**Logical/Mathematical**
out-loud problem solving, puzzles, games, outlines, strategizing

**Visual/Spatial**
pictorials, flow charts, mindmaps, timelines, models, videotapes, art work

**Bodily/Kinesthetic**
exhibitions, experiments, models, skits, manipulatives, simulations, role play

**Musical/Rhythmic**
original songs, dances, rhythmical patterning

**Interpersonal**
peer review, small group critiques, cooperative learning, leadership

**Intrapersonal**
reflective journals, goal setting, self-directed projects, self-assessment

**Naturalist**
observations, logs, categorizing, classifying, experiments

# Integrating Writing and Science

activities. Being cooperative activities, students work in groups and also access and develop their interpersonal intelligence. Additionally, students compose songs, diagram sequences, prioritize alternatives, draw pictures and much more. The multiple intelligences are incorporated throughout the activities. Each activity lists the intelligences used in the Multiple Intelligences section of the intro page.

## Higher-Level Thinking

Benjamin Bloom classified different types of thinking skills into a taxonomy, commonly known as Bloom's Taxonomy. His taxonomy of thinking skills is hierarchical. It begins with the lower levels of thinking and moves up to higher-level thinking skills. See Bloom's Taxonomy at left. Higher-Level thinking is usually considered thinking skills beyond the knowledge and comprehension levels.

Much emphasis has been placed lately on incorporating higher-level thinking in the subject areas. Writing is a helpful tool in that direction. Writing by its very nature challenges students to move beyond knowledge and comprehension.

Additionally, many of the activities were written with higher-level thinking skills in mind. Throughout the activities, students apply their knowledge to new situations, use their analytical skills as they delve into issues, pull together different information into a coherent written synthesis, and evaluate the merits of alternatives. The section called Levels of Thinking on the intro page of each activity lists the thinking skills included in the activity corresponding to Bloom's Taxonomy.

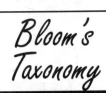

### Bloom's Taxonomy

**Higher-Level Thinking**
- 6. Evaluation
- 5. Synthesis
- 4. Analysis
- 3. Application
- 2. Comprehension
- 1. Knowledge

**Lower-Level Thinking**

### In Summary

*Integrating writing and science makes science come alive and enriches a student's understanding and appreciation of science! In this book, you will find a treasure chest of cooperative learning, multiple intelligences, higher-level thinking/writing activities to integrate writing and science!*

Virginia DeBolt: *Write! Science*
Kagan Cooperative Learning • 1 (800) WEE CO-OP

Integrating Writing and Science

# 10 Rules for Writers

1. Write.

2. Write.

3. Write Often.

4. Write about anything.

5. Write about everything.

6. Write about what you see.

7. Write about what you learn.

8. Write about what you think.

9. Write about what you read.

10. WRITE!

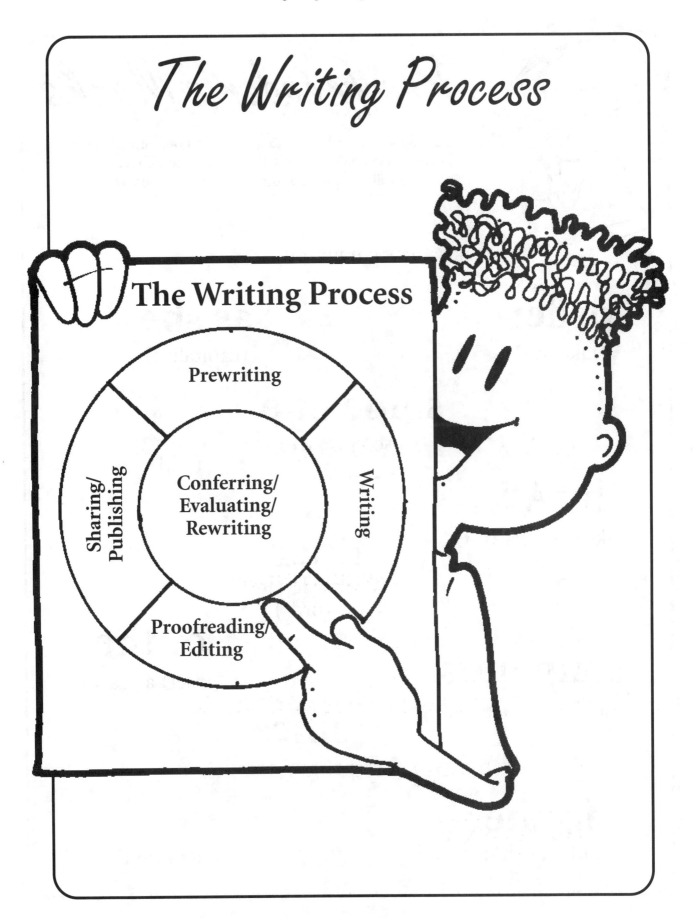

Integrating Writing and Science

# Proofreader's Marks

Use these standard marks to show corrections needed in written copy. These symbols are used so that anyone who reads the writing will interpret the corrections in the same way.

(make a new paragraph)

**order**
(take out)

**as she**
(capitalize)

**some one**
(close up space)

(add)

**by A**
(make lowercase)

**thier**
(reverse letters or words)

**onthe**
(insert a space)

**soup nuts**
(add punctuation)

**since**
(change words)

**for her**
(move as shown)

.
(add a period)

Virginia DeBolt: *Write! Science*
Kagan Cooperative Learning • 1 (800) WEE CO-OP

# Peer Conference Gambit Cards

**Directions:** Cut out the cards below. Use these sentence starters when you respond to writing.

I like the part where…

I like the way you used the word _____.

What did you mean when you said…

What happened after…

I liked your beginning because…

I would like to know more about…

I had a clear picture in my mind of the part where…

What would you lose if…

What are you going to do next?

Integrating Writing and Science

# Peer Conference Response Form

Author's Name _____

Title _____

Helper's Name _____

Date _____

I like


I want to know more about


One thing you might think about doing


Other

# Integrating Writing and Science

**Peer Response**

Title

Name

*Rough Draft*

Virginia DeBolt: *Write! Science*

# Part II

# Science Writing Activities

This section of the book consists of thirty-six detailed multiple intelligences, cooperative learning, higher-level thinking activities to assist in teaching and writing about science.

The cooperative learning structures used in this section all provide valuable learning experiences, adaptable to any type of content. These structures were selected to lead learners through various stages of thinking and writing about science. I hope your experiences using the structures in these science activities will open up other ways of applying them in your science curriculum.

For the teacher, there are specific ideas for introducing and using the activities and reproducible black-line masters which can be given to the students.

Interspersed through the activities, you will find Journal Topics pages. Journal topics are brief "just write" activities. They can be used in five or ten minutes at the start or close of the class period. The use of journals is explained in more depth on pages 6-7.

# I Want to Know

Students, like scientists, are naturally curious. In this activity, students generate questions they have about a new topic. After studying the topic, students answer their own questions. This activity creates interest and helps in deciding where students need attention or where their knowledge is already fairly solid.

*This activity is an adaptation of the K-W-L format (What do I Know? What do I Want to Learn? What have I Learned?).*

## ACTIVITY 1 — at-a-glance

**Cooperative Structure**
- Think-Write-Pair-Share

**Level of Thinking**
- Comprehension
- Application

**Multiple Intelligences**
- Verbal/Linguistic
- Interpersonal
- Intrapersonal

### Ideas for my class...
- Use this activity to introduce any new topic to the class.

### More ideas for my class...

IDEA BANK

## Think-Write-Pair-Share

Ask students to think of two questions they have regarding the topic. Give them 10-15 seconds of think time, then have them write them down on scratch paper. Students pair up to read their questions to a partner. Select a few students to share one of their own, or one of their partner's questions with the class. The questions can be recorded on the chalkboard or overhead. Keep repeating the activity until students have generated a number of questions they have about the topic. When you feel you have piqued students interest in the topic, you are ready to proceed with the unit.

## Independent Write

Have students use the left column of the I Want to Know reproducible to write the questions they are most interested in or hope to learn about in the new chapter. The paper should be handed in and stored until the chapter is completed. Then, students answer their own questions in the right column.

Virginia DeBolt: *Write! Science*

# I Want to Know

Name _____ Date _____

**Directions:** Fill in the topic in the box below. Write questions you have about the topic in the left column. Use the right column to answer your questions.

*I want to know about* _____.
                                           *topic*

| Questions | Answers |
|---|---|
|  |  |
|  |  |
|  |  |
|  |  |
|  |  |
|  |  |

# Industry & the Environment

*Human industry affects the environment. But how? For example, how does the paper industry affect the environment? The recycling industry? The oil industry? The computer industry? The fishing industry? The construction industry? The farming industry? In this activity, students brainstorm how a given industry affects the environment and write about the two most significant impacts.*

## ACTIVITY 2

### at-a-glance

**Cooperative Structure**
- 4S Brainstorming

**Level of Thinking**
- Analysis
- Synthesis

**Multiple Intelligences**
- Verbal/Linguistic
- Logical/Mathematical
- Interpersonal

### IDEA BANK

| Ideas for my class... | More ideas for my class... |
|---|---|
| **Impact of following industries on environment:** | • |
| • Local industries | • |
| • High-tech industries | • |
| • Fashion industry | • |
| • Paper industry | • |
| • Oil industry | • |
| • Fishing industry | • |
| • Construction industry | • |
| • Recycling industry | • |

## 4S Brainstorming

Group the students in teams of four. Each student needs three or four slips of paper. Give each student a role to play in the brainstorming:

- **Speed Captain:** Apply time pressure, push for speed. Research shows that creativity increases with time pressure.
- **Sergeant Support:** Encourage all ideas. Research shows that fluency increases when every contribution is praised during the brainstorming session.
- **Sultan of Silly:** Encourage silly, off-the-wall thinking. It improves creativity and may lead to an idea that works.
- **Synergy Guru:** Encourage piggy-backing of ideas.

Announce the industry that the students will explore. Follow these steps for brainstorming.

Virginia DeBolt: *Write! Science*
Kagan Cooperative Learning • 1 (800) WEE CO-OP

## Industry & the Environment

### ACTIVITY 2

1. The first student writes one idea of how the industry affects the environment on a card, says it aloud, and places it in the center of the table.
2. The next student repeats the process, with a new idea.
3. Each student continues in turn until all the papers are used.

### Independent Write

From the ideas produced during the brainstorming session, each student picks two ideas that he or she considers most significant in terms of impact on the environment. Students write about the industry's two most significant impacts on the environment.

Virginia DeBolt: *Write! Science*
Kagan Cooperative Learning • 1 (800) WEE CO-OP

# Journal Topics

- Is there another way to do the experiment?

- How did you form your hypothesis?

- What did you learn from the reading assignment?

- What questions do you have about the reading assignment?

- What message do you have for scientists working in this field?

# Evaluate the Alternatives

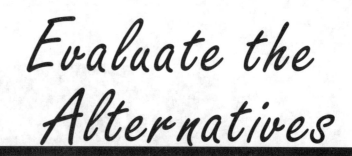

## ACTIVITY 3 at-a-glance

### Cooperative Structures
- ThinkPad Brainstorming
- RoundRobin
- RoundTable

### Level of Thinking
- Evaluation

### Multiple Intelligences
- Verbal/Linguistic
- Logical/Mathematical
- Visual/Spatial
- Interpersonal

*Protecting the environment is the subject of hundreds of articles and books. Science, ethics, politics, individual rights and other factors collide when environmental issues are raised. Automobiles, for example, might be built to run on natural gas, solar power, electrical power, even steam. Alternatives abound, but which are the right ones? In this activity, students brainstorm alternatives, discuss the advantages and disadvantages, then write an essay.*

| Ideas for my class... | More ideas for my class... |
|---|---|
| **Evaluate alternatives to:** | • |
| • Automobiles and pollution | • |
| • Paper consumption and deforestation | • |
| • Plastics and landfills | • |
| • Construction and land development | • |
|  | • |
|  | • |
|  | • |

IDEA BANK

## ThinkPad Brainstorming

Present a environmental issue to students. For example, "Automobile exhaust pollutes the air. What are some possible alternative forms of cars or transportation?" Each student brainstorms alternatives, and writes each idea or a separate thinkpad slip.

## RoundRobin

Students take turns presenting their ideas to teammates. After all ideas are presented, students select their favorite solution.

Virginia DeBolt: *Write! Science*

## Evaluate the Alternatives

**ACTIVITY 3**

### RoundTable

Each team divides a sheet of paper in half and writes "advantages" on one side and "disadvantages on the other side (see illustration). The sheet is passed around the team, each teammate adding an advantage or disadvantage to the sheet and reading it aloud to teammates.

### Independent Write

Students write about their alternative solution. The papers can be organized into four paragraphs:

**Paragraph 1:** Discuss the issue and present the alternative.
**Paragraph 2:** The advantages.
**Paragraph 3:** The disadvantages.
**Paragraph 4:** Conclusion and stance on the issue.

*Electric Cars*

| Advantages | Disadvantages |
|---|---|
|  |  |

# Evaluate the Alternatives

Name _____ Date _____

**Directions:** Fill in the environmental problem and your alternative in the box below. Write a paper evaluating your alternative. Your writing should include 1) a discussion of the problem, 2) the advantages of the alternative, 3) the disadvantages of the alternative, and 4) your conclusion on the problem and the alternative.

My alternative to _____
                              *problem*
is _____.
                              *alternative*

# Journal Topics

- What sort of control could you use for the experiment?

- What did you learn today?

- Which part of yesterday's class interested you most?

- How would you apply this to the real world?

- Relate the chapter to yourself.

# Prioritize the Problems

## ACTIVITY 4

### at-a-glance

**Cooperative Structures**
- ThinkPad Brainstorming
- Team Sort

**Level of Thinking**
- Evaluation

**Multiple Intelligences**
- Verbal/Linguistic
- Logical/Mathematical
- Visual/Spatial
- Interpersonal

Is protecting a species of fish as important as protecting a watershed? Is eliminating acid rain as important as preserving farmland? Is protecting the rainforest as important as auto emission standards? Which issue is the most crucial? In this activity, students brainstorm environment issues, prioritize them, then write a description and justification of their prioritization systems.

### IDEA BANK

| Ideas for my class... | More ideas for my class... |
|---|---|
| **Prioritize the problems:**<br>• Water quality<br>• Global warming<br>• Air quality<br>• Auto emissions<br>• Rainforest<br>• Endangered species<br>• Chemical additives in food<br>• Agricultural chemicals<br>• Land use<br>• Greenhouse effect | •<br>•<br>•<br>•<br>•<br>•<br>•<br>•<br>•<br>• |

## ThinkPad Brainstorming

Have students brainstorm as many environmental problems as they can think of or have learned about: rainforest depletion, air pollution, water pollution. Have them write each problem on an index card, thinkpad slip or post-it note. For young students, give teams a list of problems to record on index cards.

## Team Sort

The cards are distributed evenly among the team members. Tell students to group the cards into sets of related issues. Each student, in turn, places a card on the table, and announces how it connects with other cards in the same group. When all the cards are placed in groups, tell students to create a heading or label for each category.

Virginia DeBolt: *Write! Science*
Kagan Cooperative Learning • 1 (800) WEE CO-OP

## Prioritize the Problems

## ACTIVITY 4

Then, students prioritize the issues by category. Which category of related items is the most important? Less important? The least important? Students take turns prioritizing a category. A student may say, "I think pollution is the highest priority. Does everyone agree?" If students don't agree, they can vote. The next student may say, "Conservation is the next highest priority. Do we all agree?" Students move the index cards and categories to reflect their priorities.

Next, have students prioritize the individual issues within each category. Student One may say, "Do we all agree that air pollution is the biggest pollution problem?" If teammates agree, the air pollution card is placed as the first issue under the pollution category. This continues until the team has prioritized all environmental issues.

## Independent Write

Have students write a description of their prioritization decisions and a justification for why they feel some issues are more important.

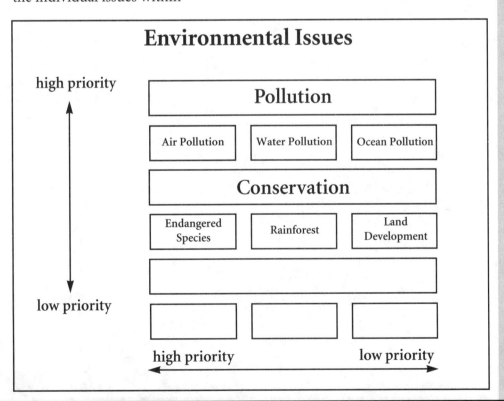

Virginia DeBolt: *Write! Science*
Kagan Cooperative Learning • 1 (800) WEE CO-OP

# Prioritize the Problems

Name _____ Date _____

**Directions:** Describe how you prioritized the problems. Then, give specific reasons why you prioritized the problems how you did.

*Describe your prioritization system* _____

_____
_____
_____
_____
_____

*Justify your prioritization system* _____

_____
_____
_____
_____
_____
_____
_____
_____
_____
_____
_____
_____
_____
_____

# Journal Topics

- How can you help the environment?

- What are the main ideas from today's lesson?

- Apply today's learning to consumer goods.

- How would today's scientific knowledge have changed World War II?

# Propose the Solution

Many environmental issues are interrelated. Reforestation not only helps reverse rainforest depletion, but also helps reverse ozone depletion. In this activity, students create a word web to help them see how three environmental issues are related, then they write a paper to the chairman of "Students Coalition on the Environment," proposing solutions.

## ACTIVITY 5

### at-a-glance

**Cooperative Structures**
- Team Word Web
- Think-Write-RoundRobin

**Level of Thinking**
- Application
- Evaluation

**Multiple Intelligences**
- Verbal/Linguistic
- Logical/Mathematical
- Visual/Spatial
- Interpersonal

| Ideas for my class... | More ideas for my class... |
|---|---|
| **Propose solutions to:** | • |
| • Acid rain | • |
| • Loss of habitat | • |
| • Air pollution | • |
| • Loss of rain forest resources | • |
| • Water depletion | • |
| • Ozone depletion | • |
| • Smog | • |
| • Species extinction | • |

**IDEA BANK**

## Team Word Web

Give each team three environmental issues or have them select their own. These are written in boxes in the center of a large paper. Team members work together using different colored markers or crayons to create a web of solutions in ovals. See sample word web.

## Think-Write-RoundRobin

After teams have finished their word webs have them answer the following reflection questions about the issues and their word web. Have them think about their responses, write them down on a scrap of paper, then share them in turn with teammates.
- How are the solutions related?
- How are the problems related?
- Does a solution create a further problem?
- Which ideas hold promise?
- What will we suggest to the committee?

Virginia DeBolt: *Write! Science*
Kagan Cooperative Learning • 1 (800) WEE CO-OP

*Propose the Solution*

## ACTIVITY 5

### Independent Write
Students write a letter suggesting solutions to the three environmental problems to the chairman of an imaginary committee called "Students Coalition on the Environment."

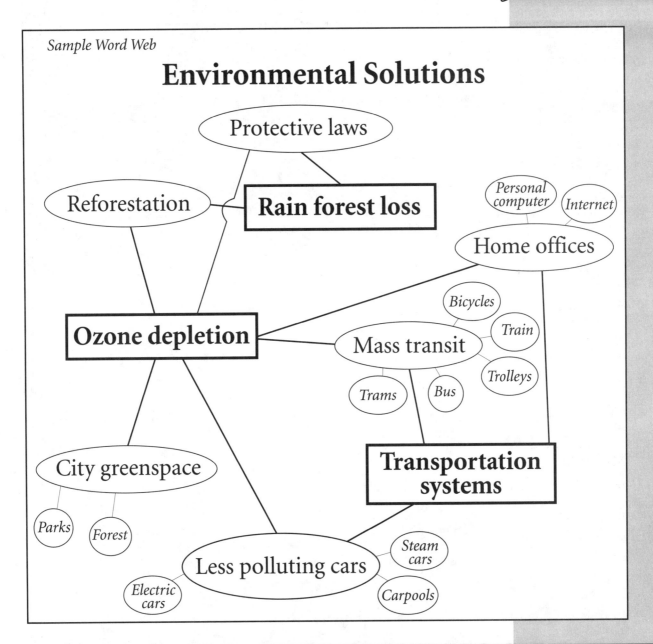

*Sample Word Web*

**Environmental Solutions**

- Protective laws
- Reforestation
- **Rain forest loss**
- Home offices — Personal computer, Internet
- **Ozone depletion**
- Mass transit — Bicycles, Train, Trolleys, Trams, Bus
- City greenspace — Parks, Forest
- **Transportation systems**
- Less polluting cars — Steam cars, Carpools, Electric cars

Virginia DeBolt: *Write! Science*
Kagan Cooperative Learning • 1 (800) WEE CO-OP

# Propose the Solution

**Name** _____ **Date** _____

**Directions:** Fill in the environmental issues in the boxes. Write a letter to the Chairman of the Students Coalition on the Environment proposing solutions to the three issues.

| issue #1 | issue #2 | issue #3 |

Dear Chairman,

_____
_____
_____
_____
_____
_____
_____
_____
_____
_____
_____
_____
_____
_____
_____
_____
_____
_____
_____

Virginia DeBolt: *Write! Science*
Kagan Cooperative Learning • 1 (800) WEE CO-OP

# Journal Topics

- What scientific knowledge affects your life?

- Write a few paragraphs using three of the vocabulary words.

- Write about a question you missed on the homework assignment.

- Write about a question you missed on the test.

# I Believe...

Many students are interested in global and national issues involving science and scientific experiments. Some may have strong opinions about things like cloning, whaling, drugs or animal testing. What is the underlying belief that engenders those opinions? In this activity, students write about their beliefs on a given topic and share it with teammates.

## ACTIVITY 6 at-a-glance

### Cooperative Structures
- Think-Pair-Share
- RoundRobin

### Level of Thinking
- Application
- Analysis

### Multiple Intelligences
- Verbal/Linguistic
- Interpersonal
- Intrapersonal

### IDEA BANK

| Ideas for my class... | More ideas for my class... |
|---|---|
| **What I believe about:** | • |
| • Cloning | • |
| • Animal testing | • |
| • Whaling | • |
| • Commercial fishing | • |
| • Genetic engineering | • |
| • Artificial intelligence | • |
| • Euthanasia | • |
| • Abortion | • |
| • Space Exploration | • |

## Think-Pair-Share

Introduce an ethical issue to the class like cloning or genetic engineering. For example, "Much progress has been made with cloning animals. Should we clone humans?"

## Independent Write

Give students some time to think about how they feel on the issue. Have them pair up and discuss their beliefs with a partner. Select a few students to share their beliefs with the class. Repeat this process two more times. Have students discuss with a new partner each time. Have students write about their beliefs on the issue on the I Believe... reproducible.

## RoundRobin

Ask students to take turns reading their belief statements aloud in their teams or in small groups. After each student reads, the listeners should praise or paraphrase in response.

Virginia DeBolt: *Write! Science*
Kagan Cooperative Learning • 1 (800) WEE CO-OP

# I Believe...

**Name** _____ **Date** _____

**Directions:** Fill in the topic in the box below. Write what you believe about the topic. Share your belief statement with teammates.

*What I believe about* _____.
                                          *ethical issue*

*I believe* _____

Virginia DeBolt: *Write! Science*
Kagan Cooperative Learning • 1 (800) WEE CO-OP

# A New Invention

Asking students to invent something elicits divergent, creative thinking and involves numerous learning modalities. In short, it is an ideal project. In this activity, students come up with an invention, then share their inventions with teammates.

## ACTIVITY 7 at-a-glance

**Cooperative Structure**
- Team Interview

**Level of Thinking**
- Application
- Analysis
- Synthesis

**Multiple Intelligences**
- Verbal/Linguistic
- Logical/Mathematical
- Visual/Spatial
- Bodily/Kinesthetic
- Interpersonal

### IDEA BANK

| Ideas for my class... | More ideas for my class... |
|---|---|
| **Invent a new:**<br>• Simple machine<br>• Form of transportation<br>• Form of communication<br>• Observation<br>• Computer<br>• Television<br>• Rocket ship | •<br>•<br>•<br>•<br>•<br>•<br>•<br>• |

## Independent Write

What the world needs is a ... what? Have students come up with a new invention related to the topic of study. For example, when studying simple machines, have students make an invention made only of levers, pulleys and inclined planes. When studying space, have students invent a new space shuttle or telescope. Using the A New Invention reproducible, have students draw their invention, give it a name and describe it.

## Team Interview

Have the students display and discuss their inventions to their teammates. Give each inventor two or three minutes to explain his or her invention. The team members then have a minute or two in which to ask "interview" questions about the invention. Finally, group members praise the inventor with gambits such as "I like the way you ..." or "This is a good idea because..."

Virginia DeBolt: *Write! Science*
Kagan Cooperative Learning • 1 (800) WEE CO-OP

# A New Invention

**Name** _____ **Date** _____

**Directions:** Draw your invention in the box below. Label your diagram if necessary. Name your invention and describe it below.

*My Invention*

*Invention Name* _____

*Description* _____

_____
_____
_____
_____
_____
_____
_____
_____
_____
_____
_____
_____

**Bonus:** Build a working model of your invention

Virginia DeBolt: *Write! Science*
Kagan Cooperative Learning • 1 (800) WEE CO-OP

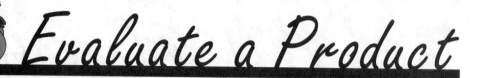

# Evaluate a Product

We wash our hair with shampoo and conditioners; we spray on perfume and cologne; we clean our clothes with laundry detergent and our dishes with dishwashing detergent. What is really in these household products and how healthy or potentially hazardous are they? In this activity, students research common household products and share their findings with classmates.

## ACTIVITY 8 at-a-glance

**Cooperative Structure**
- RoundRobin

**Level of Thinking**
- Comprehension
- Application
- Analysis
- Evaluation

**Multiple Intelligences**
- Verbal/Linguistic
- Logical/Mathematical
- Bodily/Kinesthetic
- Interpersonal

### IDEA BANK

| Ideas for my class... | More ideas for my class... |
|---|---|
| **Evaluate these products:** <br> • Hair spray <br> • Laundry detergent <br> • Deodorant <br> • Window cleaner <br> • Shaving cream <br> • Dishwashing detergent <br> • Toothpaste <br> • Soap <br> • Cologne | • <br> • <br> • <br> • <br> • <br> • <br> • <br> • <br> • |

## Independent Write

Students pick one common household product they use often like toothpaste, deodorant, dishwashing soap. They write about the intended use of the product, the ingredients, the benefits, the potential hazards, and their overall evaluation of the product. Students may use the reproducible to take notes on their products. If you have students research the ingredients and the potential hazards of their products, students will need more writing space as their resulting papers will be more elaborate.

## RoundRobin

After students have written their product evaluation, have them share them with teammates.

Students can also share their evaluations with the class using a product museum. Students bring in their products and display them along with their evaluation in the museum.

Virginia DeBolt: *Write! Science*
Kagan Cooperative Learning • 1 (800) WEE CO-OP

# Evaluate a Product

Name _____  Date _____

**Directions:** Describe and evaluate your product by filling in the information below. Select a common household product that you use frequently and fill in your product in the box below. Be prepared to share your product evaluation with teammates.

Product Name & Brand: _____
                        *product name and brand*

Intended Use: _____
_____
_____

Ingredients: _____
_____
_____
_____

Benefits: _____
_____
_____
_____

Potential Hazards: _____
_____
_____
_____

Overall Evaluation: _____
_____
_____
_____
_____
_____

# Create a Question

*Genius is defined as the ability to ask the right question. It takes clear thinking and solid information to ask a good review question. In this activity, students ask a number of review questions, and answer questions other students create. Students reflect on the questions they made up and the questions they received.*

## Activity 9 at-a-glance

**Cooperative Structure**
- Send-A-Problem

**Level of Thinking**
- Comprehension
- Application
- Evaluation

**Multiple Intelligences**
- Verbal/Linguistic
- Logical/Mathematical
- Interpersonal

### IDEA BANK

| Ideas for my class... | More ideas for my class... |
|---|---|
| **Create questions for:** <br> • Equations <br> • Reading assignment review <br> • Experimental results <br> • Chapter review <br> • Chart or graph interpretation | • <br> • <br> • <br> • <br> • <br> • <br> • <br> • |

## Send-A-Problem

Give teams note pads or index cards. Each student writes one problem or question on each card. The cards can have problems to solve or review questions from the chapter or topic. The problem is written on the front of the card, the answer on the back. Teammates then put their heads together to check the problems and answers, making sure that the problems they will send to another team are clear and accurate.

At your signal, teams send their problems to a neighboring team. Student One is the reader for the first problem and reads to the team. The team comes to consensus about the answer. Student Two is the Recorder for the first problem and writes the answer on a separate sheet of paper. The Reader turns over the problem card and the answer is checked. When every team has discussed and checked their problems, give a signal for the problems to be sent to the next team. Students rotate the roles of Reader and Recorder for the new round of work.

## Independent Write

Have students conclude the activity by reflecting on the problems they created and answered on the Create a Question reproducible.

Virginia DeBolt: *Write! Science*
Kagan Cooperative Learning • 1 (800) WEE CO-OP

# Create a Question

Name _____ Date _____

**Directions:** Fill in the topic you are studying in the box below. Write about the questions you created and the questions you answered.

| The topic we are studying is _____ . |
|---|
| *topic* |

My best question: _____
_____
_____
_____

My team's best question: _____
_____
_____
_____

The most interesting question we received: _____
_____
_____
_____

The question I learned most from: _____
_____
_____
_____

The hardest question we received: _____
_____
_____
_____
_____

Virginia DeBolt: *Write! Science*
Kagan Cooperative Learning • 1 (800) WEE CO-OP

# Internet Research

If you have "surfed the net," you know that there are all sorts of lists, web sites, and information exchanges you can access. In this activity, students hang ten on the keyboard and research a given science topic together as a team. Students write their own paper on their topic of inquiry.

## ACTIVITY 10

### at-a-glance

**Materials Needed**
• Access to the internet

**Cooperative Structures**
• Team Project
• RoundRobin

**Level of Thinking**
• Application
• Synthesis

**Multiple Intelligences**
• Verbal/Linguistic
• Logical/Mathematical
• Visual/Spatial
• Bodily/Kinesthetic
• Interpersonal

### IDEA BANK

| Ideas for my class... | More ideas for my class... |
|---|---|
| **Internet research topics:**<br>• Species of lizard found in various locations<br>• Major rock types in various locations<br>• Any topic under study currently<br>• Anatomy<br>• Weather Forecasts<br>• Animal | •<br>•<br>•<br>•<br>•<br>•<br>• |

## Team Project

Give teams a topic to research using the internet. Teams can each have a separate topic or can all research the same topic. For example, the topic may be lizards. Students work as a team at the computer. The team decides where to go to find information, what to print, and what to take notes on. Students take their own notes because they will have to write their own papers on the topic.

## Independent Write

On the reproducible, students write about what they found about their topic on the internet.

## RoundRobin

Students share their writing with teammates. If each team has a different topic, have students switch teams so that each teammate has a different topic to share.

### Alternative Activity

Have students work in teams to create a survey, then e-mail their survey for responses. E-mailed surveys can be distributed to various student-oriented newsgroups. Students write about their survey responses, including charts and graphs, if applicable.

Virginia DeBolt: *Write! Science*
Kagan Cooperative Learning • 1 (800) WEE CO-OP

# Internet Research

Name _____ Date _____

**Directions:** Fill in the topic of research in the box below. Write what you learned about your topic on the internet.

On the internet, we researched _____.
                                         *topic*

What I learned _____

# Classify This!

What are phyla or the tidy columns and rows of the periodic table but classification systems? Classifying is an essential skill for a scientist. This is a generic activity that can be used to classify anything from animals to elements. Teams develop their own classification system, and share them with other teams. Students write about their favorite system.

## ACTIVITY 11

### at-a-glance

**Cooperative Structures**
- Unstructured Sort
- Simultaneous Chalkboard Share

**Level of Thinking**
- Analysis

**Multiple Intelligences**
- Verbal/Linguistic
- Logical/Mathematical
- Visual/Spatial
- Interpersonal

### IDEA BANK

| Ideas for my class... | More ideas for my class... |
|---|---|
| **Classify This:**<br>• Vocabulary words<br>• Animals<br>• Plants<br>• Minerals<br>• Energy sources<br>• Machines<br>• Cells<br>• Systems<br>• Experimental protocols<br>• Cycles in nature | •<br>•<br>•<br>•<br>•<br>•<br>•<br>•<br>• |

## Unstructured Sort

Students record each item to be categorized on a separate card, post-it note, or thinkpad slip. For example, if students are classifying animals, the first card would say "Elephant," the second, "Tiger." Teammates work together to develop a classification system that works for all the items. The classification system can be drawn on butcher paper. The cards are then evenly divided among teammates and students take turns placing their cards in their system.

## Simultaneous Chalkboard Share

Each team works to recreate their classification system in a designated area on the chalkboard. If the classification systems are drawn on butcher paper, students can tape or glue their cards to the paper and display it in front of the class. Teams can tour the class checking out other teams classification systems.

## Independent Write

Students pick their favorite categorization system and describe why it is the best system.

Virginia DeBolt: *Write! Science*

# Classify This!

Name _____ Date _____

**Directions:** Draw your favorite categorization system in the box below. Describe why you think it is the best.

*I think this system is the best because* _____

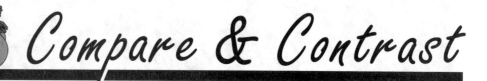

# Compare & Contrast

The ability to compare and contrast is one of the most fundamental thinking skills of the scientist. In this activity, students develop this capacity as they compare and contrast scientific concepts with regard to specific characteristics. Students use this exercise as the basis for a compare and contrast paper.

## Activity 12 at-a-glance

**Cooperative Structure**
- Pair Project

**Level of Thinking**
- Analysis

**Multiple Intelligences**
- Verbal/Linguistic
- Visual/Spatial
- Interpersonal

## Idea Bank

**Ideas for my class...**

Compare and Contrast:
- Weight/mass
- Kinetic/potential energy
- Water cycle/oxygen cycle
- Plants/animals
- Cells/organs
- Photosynthesis/metabolism
- Igneous/sedimentary rocks
- Liquids/gases

**More ideas for my class...**
- 
- 
- 
- 
- 
- 
- 
- 

## Pair Project

The secret of a successful compare-and-contrast essay is to write about selected features of the two subjects. For example, a student might compare and contrast animals and plants. A well-organized essay would look at the specific features of animals and compare and contrast them to the corresponding feature of plants like reproduction, movement, food sources. (See graphic).

Give students the topics to compare and contrast. Using the Compare & Contrast reproducible have students work in pairs to come up with how the two objects are similar and how they are different with respect to specific characteristics.

## Independent Write

Students can turn their graphic organizer into an interesting paper. Have them begin with an introduction, write a paragraph detailing the likenesses and differences in each of the items compared on the graphic, and finish with a brief summary.

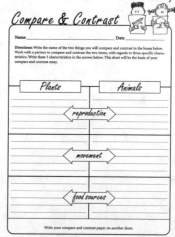

Virginia DeBolt: *Write! Science*
Kagan Cooperative Learning • 1 (800) WEE CO-OP

# Compare & Contrast

Name _____  Date _____

**Directions:** Write the name of the two things you will compare and contrast in the boxes below. Work with a partner to compare and contrast the two items, with regards to three specific characteristics. Write these three characteristics in the arrows below. This sheet will be the basis of your compare-and-contrast essay.

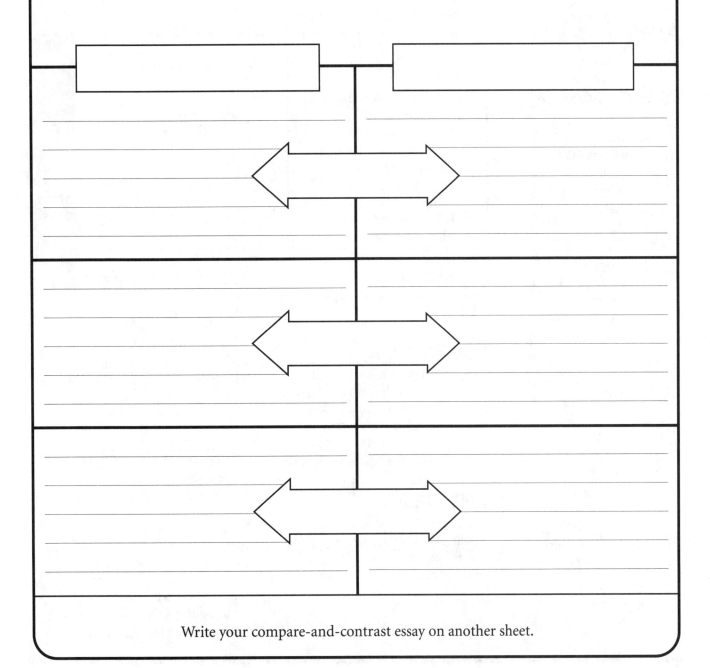

Write your compare-and-contrast essay on another sheet.

Virginia DeBolt: *Write! Science*
Kagan Cooperative Learning • 1 (800) WEE CO-OP

# The Advantages and Disadvantages

## ACTIVITY 13
### at-a-glance

Profound scientific questions face us now and in the future. What are the ethics of progress, of discovery? How do we weigh possible harm against possible gain? Learning to evaluate advantages and disadvantages is a crucial decision-making skill. In this activity, students brainstorm the advantages and disadvantages of any given item, then write an essay.

### Cooperative Structures

- ThinkPad Brainstorming
- RoundRobin
- Team Discussion

### Level of Thinking

- Analysis
- Evaluation

### Multiple Intelligences

- Verbal/Linguistic
- Logical/Mathematical
- Visual/Spatial
- Interpersonal
- Intrapersonal

### IDEA BANK

| Ideas for my class... | More ideas for my class... |
|---|---|
| **What are the advantages & disadvantages of:**<br>• Nuclear energy<br>• Gene manipulation<br>• Chemotherapy<br>• Protecting endangered species<br>• Internet access<br>• Animal testing<br>• Space exploration<br>• Laser surgery | •<br>•<br>•<br>•<br>•<br>•<br>•<br>• |

## ThinkPad Brainstorming

Give students a topic like nuclear energy. Have them work in teams of four to brainstorm as many possible advantages and disadvantages as they can come up with. Students record each idea on a separate think pad slip.

## RoundRobin

Students take turns sharing their advantages and disadvantages with teammates. Students place their ideas on the advantages side or disadvantages side of the table.

## Team Discussion

After seeing all the ideas displayed in the center of the table, teammates discuss any new ideas that come from the synergy of seeing all the advantages and disadvantages together.

## Independent Write

Tell students to write about the advantages and disadvantages of the given topic. In the written work, students need only list three advantages and three disadvantages. However, each of these three should be explained and enlarged with specific examples. After the students have weighed both sides of the problem, they should draw a conclusion and take a position.

Virginia DeBolt: *Write! Science*
Kagan Cooperative Learning • 1 (800) WEE CO-OP

# The Advantages and Disadvantages

Name _____  Date _____

**Directions:** Fill in the topic in the box below. Write about the advantages and disadvantages. Your writing should include: 1) a discussion of the topic and its importance, 2) three advantages, 3) three disadvantages, and 4) your conclusion on the issue.

*What are the advantages and disadvantages of* _____.
                                                                  topic

Virginia DeBolt: *Write! Science*

# Chart the Steps

A well-designed graphic organizer can feed a well-organized piece of writing. In this activity, students graphically depict the steps involved in a science process, then use their graphics to describe the process in writing.

## ACTIVITY 14 at-a-glance

### Materials Needed
• Rulers and other drawing materials

### Cooperative Structures
• Pair Project
• RoundRobin

### Level of Thinking
• Analysis

### Multiple Intelligences
• Verbal/Linguistic
• Logical/Mathematical
• Visual/Spatial
• Interpersonal

## IDEA BANK

| Ideas for my class... | More ideas for my class... |
|---|---|
| **Chart the steps of:**<br>• Life cycle of slime molds<br>• Four phases of matter<br>• Carbon cycle<br>• Electricity generation<br>• Cell division<br>• Aluminum production & reuse<br>• Energy changes<br>• Experiment<br>• Research project | •<br>•<br>•<br>•<br>•<br>•<br>•<br>•<br>• |

## Pair Project

Give students a science topic that involves multiple steps or a process. Cell division or the water cycle are two good examples. Have students work in pairs to graphically depict the process. You may want to show students different graphic organizers that may be helpful. See sample graphic organizers on the following page. Pairs can work out the specifics of what happens at the various stages. If helpful, students can add illustrations to their diagrams.

## Independent Write

On the Chart the Steps reproducible, students independently recreate the graphic organizer, then provide a written description of the scientific process.

## RoundRobin

Students share their writing in turn with teammates.

Virginia DeBolt: *Write! Science*
Kagan Cooperative Learning • 1 (800) WEE CO-OP

*Chart the Steps* — ACTIVITY 14

# Sample Graphic Organizers

## Cycle Graphs
Cycle graphs show chronological order or interrelationship:

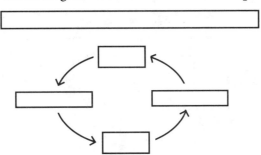

## Flow Charts
Flow chart diagrams show sequence. Standard symbols are:

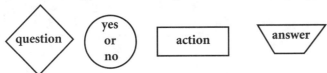

## Central Idea Graphs
Central idea graphs show parts of a whole, results of an event

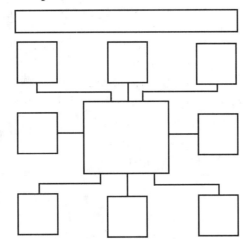

Virginia DeBolt: *Write! Science*
Kagan Cooperative Learning • 1 (800) WEE CO-OP

# Chart the Steps

Name _____ Date _____

**Directions:** Fill in the science topic in the box below. Chart the steps of the process in the box. Write a description of the chart, giving the steps in sequence.

The steps of _____.
               *science process*

Chart the steps of the process

Describe the process in writing _____
_____
_____
_____
_____
_____
_____
_____

# Journal Topics

- What are two intelligent choices you could make using today's topic?

- Write a letter to a parent about class today.

- Relate today's lesson to other science topics.

- Tell which single fact from today's class is the most important.

# A Scientific Breakthrough

*Science is a field loaded with awesome discoveries and achievements that have altered our perceptions of the world and our daily behaviors. In this activity, students pretend they are present during a scientific breakthrough or discovery, and send a telegram to a friend describing the event.*

## ACTIVITY 15

### at-a-glance

**Cooperative Structure**
- Team Interview

**Level of Thinking**
- Comprehension
- Application

**Multiple Intelligences**
- Verbal/Linguistic
- Logical/Mathematical
- Musical/Rhythmic
- Interpersonal

### IDEA BANK

| Ideas for my class... | More ideas for my class... |
|---|---|
| **Describe the scientific breakthrough:**<br>• Pasteur's discovery of pasteurization<br>• Salk's discovery of polio vaccine<br>• Edison's invention of the record player<br>• Marconi's invention of the radio | •<br>•<br>•<br>•<br>•<br>•<br>•<br>• |

## Independent Write

Tell students to pretend that they are present during a historical scientific discovery or breakthrough. Students can all be given the same discovery to write about or can each write about different events. For example, have them pretend to witness Armstrong step foot on the moon. Students write a telegram to a friend describing the event and the implications for the world. Students can use their text or other sources to include pertinent information. Tell them to be ready to share their telegram with teammates.

## Team Interview

Have students read their telegrams to their teammates. After hearing the telegram, teammates take turns asking the writer relevant interview questions for two minutes.

Virginia DeBolt: *Write! Science*
Kagan Cooperative Learning • 1 (800) WEE CO-OP

# A Scientific Breakthrough

Name _____  Date _____

**Directions:** Fill in the scientific breakthrough in the box below. Imagine you were present at the scene of this great scientific discovery or achievement. Write a telegram to a friend describing the discovery.

The scientific breakthrough _____.

## Telegram

**SEND TO:**

| Name | |
|---|---|
| Address | |
| City | State | Zip |

Filing Time: ____
Date: ____
Time Sent: ____

Message:

_____
_____
_____
_____
_____
_____
_____
_____
_____
_____
_____
_____
_____

**FROM:**

| Signature | | Name | |
|---|---|---|---|
| Sender's address | | | |
| City | | State | Zip |
| Telephone | | | |

Virginia DeBolt: *Write! Science*

# Graphic Conclusions

*Science texts and articles are fond of charts, graphs, tables, and diagrams. Why are they put in the text? What do they mean? What conclusions can be drawn? In this activity, students analyze what the graphics mean and share their analysis with teammates.*

## ACTIVITY 16 at-a-glance

### Materials Needed
- Use either a chart or a table from the text for this exercise.

### Cooperative Structure
- RoundRobin

### Level of Thinking
- Evaluation
- Analysis

### Multiple Intelligences
- Verbal/Linguistic
- Logical/Mathematical
- Visual/Spatial
- Interpersonal

### IDEA BANK

| Ideas for my class... | More ideas for my class... |
|---|---|
| **Analyze the graphic:**<br>• Periodic chart<br>• Any graph in text<br>• Animal kingdom charts<br>• Any table in text<br>• Charts of cycles<br>• Illustrations | •<br>•<br>•<br>•<br>•<br>•<br>•<br>•<br>• |

## Independent Write

Have students examine a particular table, chart, graph or diagram in the text. Tell them to analyze it carefully and write about: What does it represent? What are some interesting features? What conclusions can you draw?

## RoundRobin

After students have finished analyzing and evaluating the graphic, they share their writing with teammates.

Virginia DeBolt: *Write! Science*
Kagan Cooperative Learning • 1 (800) WEE CO-OP

# Graphic Conclusions

Name _____ Date _____

**Directions:** Fill in the title or topic of the graphic in the box below. Answer the following questions about the graph. Be prepared to share your answers with teammates.

| Graphic title or topic _____ |

What does the graphic represent? _____
_____
_____
_____

What are some interesting features about the graphic? _____
_____
_____
_____
_____

What conclusions can you draw from this graphic? Provide evidence. _____
_____
_____
_____
_____

Does the graphic help support the text? _____
_____
_____
_____
_____

Virginia DeBolt: *Write! Science*
Kagan Cooperative Learning • 1 (800) WEE CO-OP

# Science News Report

Dissection reveals digestive system! Scientist creates chemical change! In this activity, students write a newspaper article on any science topic. Students work together to collect all the necessary information, then write their own articles.

## Activity 17 at-a-glance

**Cooperative Structures**
- Think-Write-Pair-Share
- RoundRobin

**Level of Thinking**
- Comprehension
- Application
- Analysis

**Multiple Intelligences**
- Verbal/Linguistic
- Logical/Mathematical
- Interpersonal
- Visual/Spatial

### IDEA BANK

| Ideas for my class... | More ideas for my class... |
|---|---|
| **Write an article about:**<br>• Lab results<br>• Chapter summary<br>• A science discovery<br>• News from an unusual perspective such as that of earth, the air, or a microorganism | •<br>•<br>•<br>•<br>•<br>•<br>•<br>• |

## Think-Write-Pair-Share

Have each student pull out a sheet of paper and divide it into five parts. Have them label the page with the 5 W's: Who, What, Where, When, Why. See illustration below. Announce the topic you are studying, like electricity. Then have students think about "Who" was involved, who is now involved and who will be involved in the future. Have students record their ideas on the 5 W's sheet. Then, have students pair up and share their ideas with a partner. Partners can get additional ideas from each other. Pick a few students to share their ideas with the class. Students can record additional ideas. Repeat this process with the remaining 4 W's.

## Independent Write

After the Think-Write-Pair-Share, students should have lots of notes on the topic that they can use to write their newspaper article.

Students write a headline, create a graphic and a story including all 5 W's.

| Electricity |
|---|
| Who |
| What |
| Where |
| When |
| Why |

## RoundRobin

Students can share their articles with teammates.

Virginia DeBolt: *Write! Science*
Kagan Cooperative Learning • 1 (800) WEE CO-OP

# Science News Report

**Name** _____ **Date** _____

**Directions:** Write a newspaper story about a science topic. Give your newspaper a name. Include a headline, graphic and your byline.

*Newspaper Name*

*Headline*

*Graphic*

*Byline*

# Science Log

Possibly the most important writing a scientist does is keep a log of his or her activities and experiments. When you are doing lab or field work, have students use this little log book to keep a record of their work. Have students share their logs with a partner. Select a few students to share with the class.

## ACTIVITY 18 at-a-glance

**Cooperative Structure**
- Write-Pair-Share

**Level of Thinking**
- Comprehension
- Application

**Multiple Intelligences**
- Verbal/Linguistic
- Interpersonal

### IDEA BANK

| Ideas for my class... | More ideas for my class... |
|---|---|
| **Keep a log on:** | • |
| • Weather | • |
| • Plants | • |
| • Surveys | • |
| • Electricity experiments | • |
| • Organisms | • |
| • Labs | • |
| • Field studies | • |
| • Experiments | • |
|  | • |

## Independent Write

As an ongoing activity during the course of a lab or lesson, have students keep notes in the science log. The reproducible folds into a mini science log. See illustration additions or corrections to the logs. Ask two or three students to share with the whole class.

## Write-Pair-Share

For the last few minutes of class each day during the lab, have students complete the writing in their science log. Students then pair to read their entry aloud to a partner. After reading and a brief discussion, students may make

Virginia DeBolt: *Write! Science*
Kagan Cooperative Learning • 1 (800) WEE CO-OP

## Science Log

Topic _____
Name _____
Date _____

---

Date _____

Vocabulary _____
_____
_____

Main ideas _____
_____
_____
_____
_____

Data _____
_____
_____

Lab Work _____
_____
_____
_____
_____

---

(upper panels — inverted/fold-over sections)

Date _____

Vocabulary _____

Main ideas _____

Data _____

Lab Work _____

---

Date _____

Vocabulary _____

Main ideas _____

Data _____

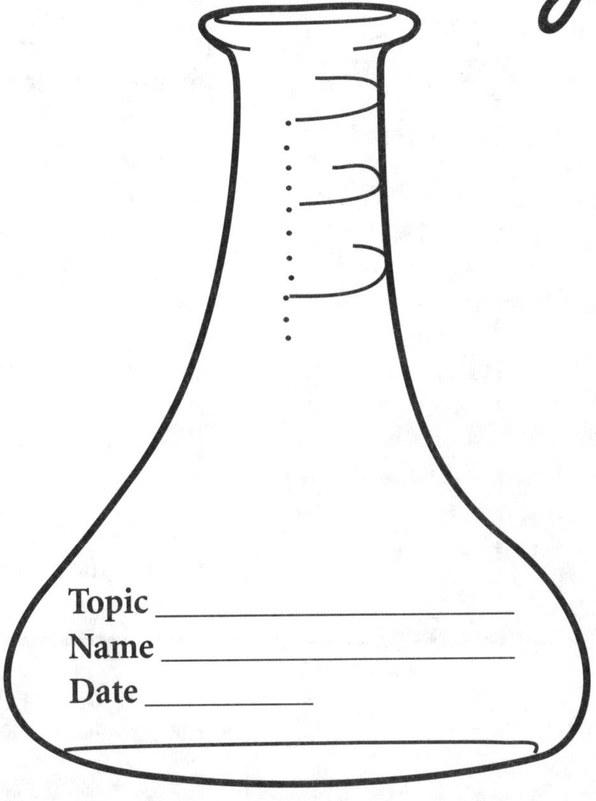

Lab Work _____

*fold here*

# Interviews About You

Birth, growth and development are science topics that we all have personal experience with. Make a connection between these topics and students' own lives with this writing activity. In this activity, students interview parents or caregivers about their own birth, growth and development, write out their interviews, then work with teammates to polish their interviews.

**Acknowledgement:** Thanks to Karen Green, science teacher at Murchison Middle School, Austin, Texas for this activity.

## ACTIVITY 19 at-a-glance

### Cooperative Structures
- 4S Brainstorming
- RoundRobin
- Simultaneous RoundTable

### Level of Thinking
- Knowledge
- Application
- Analysis
- Synthesis

### Multiple Intelligences
- Verbal/Linguistic
- Bodily/Kinesthetic
- Interpersonal
- Intrapersonal

## IDEA BANK

| Ideas for my class... | More ideas for my class... |
|---|---|
| Interviews in:<br>• Birth<br>• Growth<br>• Parenting<br>• Expert in the field<br>• Science-related jobs | •<br>•<br>•<br>•<br>•<br>•<br>•<br>•<br>• |

## 4S Brainstorming

In teams, students come up with interview questions about the topic to ask parents or caregivers. Students each record questions they would like to ask. For example, on the topic of birth, students may come up with questions like, "How much did I weigh when I was born?"

## Independent Write

Using the questions students generate in the brainstorming session, students interview their parent(s) or caregiver(s) to obtain information about their own birth, growth, development. Students can take notes or even record the interview. Students then write out a first draft of their interview.

## RoundRobin

Each student reads his or her first draft to teammates. Teammates offer comments on content (organization, clarity, meaning). See page 4 for more information on peer conferencing and for helpful forms.

Virginia DeBolt: *Write! Science*
Kagan Cooperative Learning • 1 (800) WEE CO-OP

*Interviews About You* — ACTIVITY 19

## Independent Write
Students rewrite their interviews based on teammates' feedback.

## Simultaneous RoundTable
Teammates pass the second draft of their interview clockwise for a teammate to edit. When done, students pass papers clockwise again for the text teammate to edit. In a team of four, each paper will be proofread by three students before it returns to its owner. Have students use the proofreader's marks on page 16 to edit each other's papers.

# Sample Interview Questions

### Birth
- Can you tell me about my birth? Was I on time? How did it go in the hospital while I was being born?
- Can you remember what you said when you saw me for the first time?
- How did you pick a name for me?
- What was my birth weight, length, eye color, hair color …?
- Were you okay with the fact that I am a girl/boy?
- Who was at the hospital, or in our home, awaiting my arrival?

### Growth
- What kinds of things do you remember about me during my infancy (one to twelve months)?
- What kinds of things do you remember about me during my toddler time (thirteen months to three years)?
- Was I excited about preschool and/or kindergarten? Explain.
- Talk about my early school years. What were my accomplishments, challenges, fears, confidences?

### Parenting
- What advice do you have to give me about parenting, should I decide, many years from now, that I want to be a parent?
- What is the most difficult part about parenting? The easiest part?

Virginia DeBolt: *Write! Science*
Kagan Cooperative Learning • 1 (800) WEE CO-OP

# Define This!

If you have ever tried to define a word quickly you know it may be a difficult task. It requires careful thought and exacting word choice. In this activity, students progress through a series of steps to write definitions for science vocabulary words.

## ACTIVITY 20 at-a-glance

**Cooperative Structure**
- Pairs Check

**Level of Thinking**
- Application

**Multiple Intelligences**
- Verbal/Linguistic
- Interpersonal
- Intrapersonal

### IDEA BANK

| Ideas for my class... | More ideas for my class... |
|---|---|
| • Use the major concepts from a chapter<br>• Ecosystem<br>• Biome<br>• Photosynthesis<br>• Adaptation<br>• System<br>• Force<br>• Electron<br>• Metamorphic<br>• Evolution | •<br>•<br>•<br>•<br>•<br>•<br>•<br>•<br>• |

## Pairs Check

To define science vocabulary words, students progress through the eight simple steps of Pairs Check.

**Step 1. Pair Work.** Student A in the pair works on defining the first word. Student B coaches and provides help if help is requested.

**Step 2. Coach Checks.** The coach checks his or her partner's definition for agreement. If the partners don't agree on a definition, they may ask the other pair on the team.

**Step 3. Coach Praises.** If the partners agree on a definition, the Coach offers a praiser.

**Steps 4-6. Partners Switch Roles.** Student B writes a definition while Student A coaches. The Coach checks the definition and offers a praiser when he or she agrees on the definition.

**Step 7. Pairs Check.** The team reunites and compares definitions. If they disagree and cannot reach consensus, they check the text or a dictionary. If they still can't agree, all four hands go up.

**Step 8. Team Celebrates.** If the team agrees on the definition, they congratulate each other.

Students repeat this process for every set of two words they define.

Virginia DeBolt: *Write! Science*
Kagan Cooperative Learning • 1 (800) WEE CO-OP

# Define This!

Name _____ Date _____

**Directions:** Fill in the vocabulary words in the boxes below. Write a definition for each word. Be as clear and complete as possible. Put a check in the box when your team agrees on the definition.

Word _____ ☐
Definition _____
_____
_____

Word _____ ☐
Definition _____
_____
_____

Word _____ ☐
Definition _____
_____
_____

Word _____ ☐
Definition _____
_____
_____

# Science Books

Books are filled with the wonders of the world, just waiting to be discovered by the reader. The process of actually creating a book is usually a collaborative journey through the stages of writing. In this activity, teams research a given science topic and write a team book on the topic. Each student contributes to the book. Teammates work together to edit each other's contributions. When done, teams share their books with other teams.

## ACTIVITY 21 at-a-glance

**Cooperative Structures**
- Team Discussion
- RoundRobin
- Simultaneous RoundTable
- Team Project
- Teams Present

**Level of Thinking**
- Application
- Synthesis

**Multiple Intelligences**
- Verbal/Linguistic
- Logical/Mathematical
- Visual/Spatial
- Bodily/Kinesthetic
- Interpersonal

## IDEA BANK

| Ideas for my class... | More ideas for my class... |
|---|---|
| **Write a book on:**<br>• Magnetism<br>• Amphibians<br>• Rocks<br>• Soap bubbles<br>• Your respiratory system<br>• Solar energy<br>• Hurricanes/tornadoes<br>• Simple machines<br>• Flowers<br>• Oxygen | •<br>•<br>•<br>•<br>•<br>•<br>•<br>•<br>•<br>• |

## Team Discussion

Students are assigned a book topic. For example the topic may be reptiles. The team meets to research and discuss the main topics they want to cover, and the type of book they want to create. For example, the team may decide to make a reference book, describing a different reptile on each page. Students divide the work between themselves, each researching a different reptile. It is important to tell students before the discussion that they must divide the book into sections. Students must research and write their sections separately.

## Independent Write

Students work independently to write their section(s) of the book. The reproducible can be used for the final draft. Students may write the first draft on a separate sheet of paper. As students work on their first draft, they decide which graphic to add to their section, but don't actually illustrate it until after the final draft is complete.

Virginia DeBolt: *Write! Science*
Kagan Cooperative Learning • 1 (800) WEE CO-OP

# Science Books

## RoundRobin

Students read their first draft to teammates in turn for initial content feedback. The peer response forms in the back of Part I may be helpful. If there are substantial comments, students may do a second draft, and meet again, or work on one student's contribution.

## Simultaneous RoundTable

When students are comfortable with the content of each other's paper, they work on the mechanics. Students rotate papers and all simultaneous check one teammate's work for spelling, grammar, punctuation, capitalization. The Proofreader's Marks on page 16 will be helpful. Students rotate papers, and edit the next teammate's paper. When done, each paper will be proofread three times.

## Independent Write

Students write their final drafts, then add their illustration(s).

## Team Project

Teams work on the front and back covers of their book and bind their book with a staple or hole punch the spine and use string or yarn.

## Teams Present

Teams share their book with another team or with the class. Each student reads his or her own contribution to the book. Books can also be shared with other classes or grade levels.

# Science Books

Name _____  Date _____

Book Topic _____

Section _____

74    Virginia DeBolt: *Write! Science*
Kagan Cooperative Learning • 1 (800) WEE CO-OP

# Journal Topics

- Write five questions you would ask your favorite scientist.

- What experiment does this chapter suggest to you?

- Set up a table or graph as a review of the chapter.

- Use three vocabulary words in a scientifically correct paragraph.

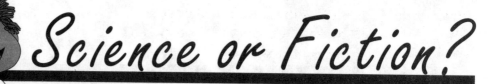

# Science or Fiction?

For many centuries and in many cultures, people have used questionable medical practices including using leeches, herbs, animal extracts and even dirt. For years, alchemists mixed metals to come up with gold. Astrologists attribute numerous phenomena to the cosmos. Are these practices science or fictions? In this activity, students explore the scientific basis for such practices.

## ACTIVITY 22 at-a-glance

**Cooperative Structures**
- Pair Project
- Pairs Present

**Level of Thinking**
- Application
- Analysis
- Evaluation

**Multiple Intelligences**
- Verbal/Linguistic
- Logical/Mathematical
- Interpersonal

## IDEA BANK

| Ideas for my class... | More ideas for my class... |
|---|---|
| **Are the following science or fiction?** <br>• Alchemy <br>• Astrology <br>• Holistic healing <br>• Acupuncture <br>• Chiropractics <br>• Aroma therapy <br>• Herbal Medicine <br>• Phrenology <br>• Psychosomatic medicine | • <br>• <br>• <br>• <br>• <br>• <br>• <br>• <br>• |

## Pair Project

Students work in pairs to research their topic. Students can take notes from the text or provided materials. This activity provides a great opportunity for students to do library research on a topic of interest. Partners decide whether the practice is a science or a fiction. Pairs write a persuasive paper arguing that the practice is a science or fiction, supporting their claim with scientific evidence. The paper is written like a newspaper article, for the fictitious newspaper, The World of Science. Partners decide on and draw an illustration for their article.

## Pairs Present

When completed, have pairs share their findings with other pairs or with the class as a presentation.

Virginia DeBolt: *Write! Science*
Kagan Cooperative Learning • 1 (800) WEE CO-OP

**Directions:** Decide whether the practice is a science or fiction. Write a newspaper article supporting your claim with scientific evidence.

## The World of Science

# News...

by _____

*illustration*

Virginia DeBolt: *Write! Science*
Kagan Cooperative Learning • 1 (800) WEE CO-OP

77

# How Does This Thing Work?

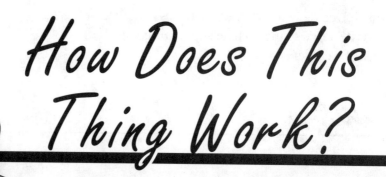

## Activity 23 at-a-glance

**Cooperative Structure**
- RoundRobin

**Level of Thinking**
- Comprehension
- Application

**Multiple Intelligences**
- Verbal/Linguistic
- Logical/Mathematical
- Visual/Spatial
- Bodily/Kinesthetic
- Interpersonal

We take appliances, machines, and electronic devices for granted. Take your television for instance. You turn it on and programs magically appear in full color with sound. How does it work? In this activity, students explore how things work.

## Idea Bank

| Ideas for my class... | More ideas for my class... |
|---|---|
| **Describe how it works**<br>• Computer<br>• X-Ray<br>• Television<br>• Telephone<br>• Smoke Detector<br>• Electricity<br>• CD Player<br>• Airplane<br>• Clock | •<br>•<br>•<br>•<br>•<br>•<br>•<br>•<br>•<br>• |

## Independent Write

Have students research an appliance, machine, or electrical device, or any science product or process under study. See ideas above. Students write a description of the item and how it works. The description should include an illustration of the product or how it works. David Macaulay's book, *The Way Things Work* is a good example of a visual guide integrated with text.

## RoundRobin

Students share their findings with teammates. If you have students explore different products, you can compile them into a reference guide that students may examine on their free time.

Virginia DeBolt: *Write! Science*
Kagan Cooperative Learning • 1 (800) WEE CO-OP

# How Does This Thing Work?

Name _____ Date _____

**Directions:** Fill in the name of your machine in the box below. Write a description and draw an illustration showing how it works. Share your machine with teammates.

| illustration | How _____ |
|---|---|
| | works.          *machine* |

How it works

_____
_____
_____
_____
_____
_____
_____
_____
_____
_____
_____
_____
_____
_____
_____
_____
_____
_____
_____
_____

Virginia DeBolt: *Write! Science*
Kagan Cooperative Learning • 1 (800) WEE CO-OP

# Concept Mobile

*Presenting and explaining information are two communication tasks essential for any professional, including scientists. In this activity, students create a mobile illustrating scientific concepts, write a description of the mobile and the science topic and then present it to the class.*

## ACTIVITY 24

### at-a-glance

**Materials Needed**
- Clothes hangers or other objects suitable for mobiles
- String, glue, scissors
- Hole punch, brads, tagboard or construction paper

**Cooperative Structures**
- Team Project
- Independent Write
- Teams Present

**Level of Thinking**
- Application
- Analysis

**Multiple Intelligences**
- Verbal/Linguistic
- Logical/Mathematical
- Visual/Spatial
- Bodily/Kinesthetic
- Interpersonal

## IDEA BANK

| Ideas for my class... | More ideas for my class... |
|---|---|
| **Create a mobile on:** | • |
| • Human/bird skeletons | • |
| • Newton's laws | • |
| • Forms of energy | • |
| • Mineral classification | • |
| • Weather types | • |
| • Endangered species | • |
| • Solar system | • |
| • Elements | • |

## Team Project

Teams of four work together to construct a mobile illustrating a scientific concept. To make sure everyone participates, have the team discuss what the mobile should look like, then decide who is to do what. For example, if the mobile is on types of natural disasters, each student may work on a different natural disaster.

## Independent Write

After the mobile is completed, students write individual explanations of their team's mobile.

## Teams Present

Teams plan, rehearse, and present their mobile to the class or to another team. Each team member must have an active role in the presentation. Each student writes out his or her part of the presentation on a separate sheet of paper in preparation, and can turn in the written description of his or her part of the presentation for a grade. Mobiles can be hung above team seating areas.

Virginia DeBolt: *Write! Science*

# Concept Mobile

Name _____ Date _____

**Directions:** Fill in the topic of your mobile in the box below. After your team has completed the mobile, describe it in depth below.

*The topic of our mobile is* _____.
*mobile topic*

# Make A Myth

Myths are traditional stories of unknown origin used to explain how the world came to be, how human and animal creatures came to possess various characteristics, and why the stars travel across the sky in meaningful patterns. These fictitious stories usually involve the exploits of gods and heroes. In this activity, students write their own myths about a science topic. This activity provides a good anticipatory set to learning the reality behind any science topic.

**ACTIVITY 25**

## at-a-glance

### Cooperative Structures
- Think-Write-RoundRobin
- RoundRobin

### Level of Thinking
- Application
- Synthesis

### Multiple Intelligences
- Verbal/Linguistic
- Logical/Mathematical
- Visual/Spatial
- Interpersonal
- Intrapersonal

## IDEA BANK

| Ideas for my class... | More ideas for my class... |
|---|---|
| **Write a myth explaining:** | • |
| • Why the sky is blue | • |
| • Why dogs bark | • |
| • Why constellations appear as they do | • |
| • Why the sun sets | • |
| • Why the moon has craters | • |
| • Why gravity holds us down | • |

## Think-Write-RoundRobin

It may be helpful to share a myth or two with the class before you begin this activity. Then, present the natural phenomena to be studied to the class as a question. For example, if the topic is earthquakes, ask the class to come up with fictitious ideas for "Where do earthquakes come from?" Give students 10-15 seconds of think time, then have them write their answers independently. Students share their ideas with teammates. Students can do several rounds to generate lots of ideas.

## Independent Write

Students independently write their own myth using their favorite idea generated.

## RoundRobin

Students in turn read their myth to teammates. After this activity, students learn the real explanation of the scientific phenomenon.

Virginia DeBolt: *Write! Science*
Kagan Cooperative Learning • 1 (800) WEE CO-OP

# Make A Myth

**Name** _____ **Date** _____

**Directions:** Fill in the topic of your myth in the box below. Create an original myth about your topic. Show your myth with your teammates.

*A myth about* _____ .
*myth topic*

# Animal Adaptations

Urbanization spells doom for the species that cannot adapt and survive in the new environment. Hawks, foxes, deer and other animals have found ways to live in a city environment. Falcons, for example, nest high above the city on the ledges and niches of skyscrapers. In this activity, students explore adaptation different animals have made or would need to make with urbanization.

## ACTIVITY 26 at-a-glance

### Materials Needed
- Large paper
- Colored pens, pencils or crayons

### Cooperative Structures
- Corners
- Pair Discussion
- RoundRobin

### Level of Thinking
- Evaluation
- Application

### Multiple Intelligences
- Verbal/Linguistic
- Logical/Mathematical
- Naturalist

## IDEA BANK

| Ideas for my class... | More ideas for my class... |
|---|---|
| **What adaptation would be necessary for:**<br>• Birds of prey<br>• Field birds<br>• Rodents<br>• Insects<br>• Lions<br>• Tigers<br>• Bears | •<br>•<br>•<br>•<br>•<br>•<br>•<br>• |

## Corners

In each of the four corners of the classroom, tape up a category of animal: birds, mammals, reptiles, amphibians. Ask students to write the name of the animal that interests them the most on a scrap of paper. Then have students go to the appropriate corner for their selected animal. In the corner, students look for a partner who is interested in the same animal as they are. For example, in the mammal corner, two students interested in lions may pair up. If students cannot find a partner who is interested in their first choice, they may have to compromise and pick another animal of interest.

## Pair Discussion

Pairs work together to discuss how urbanization has or how it would affect their animal. What adaptation would their animal need to make to survive in the city?

## Independent Write

Students write about their animal adaptations.

## RoundRobin

Students share their essays in turn with teammates.

Virginia DeBolt: *Write! Science*
Kagan Cooperative Learning • 1 (800) WEE CO-OP

# Animal Adaptations

Name _____  Date _____

**Directions:** Fill in the name of your animal in the box below. Write what adaptations your animal needed or would need to make to survive in an urban environment.

*The adaptations of* _____
*with urbanization.*           *animal*

# Outline Review

Outlining is one of the, if not the, most helpful tools for writing and studying. By outlining, students examine main concepts, supporting details, and the interrelations of the learning materials. In this activity, students outline a chapter or parts of the text. Team members use their outlines to recreate a summary of the chapter or text.

## ACTIVITY 27
### at-a-glance

**Materials Needed**
- Scissors

**Cooperative Structure**
- RoundTable

**Level of Thinking**
- Comprehension
- Application

**Multiple Intelligences**
- Verbal/Linguistic
- Interpersonal

### Idea Bank

| Ideas for my class... | More ideas for my class... |
|---|---|
| **Create an outline of:**<br>• The current chapter<br>• Chapters covered in the semester exam<br>• An experiment<br>• A presentation<br>• A lesson<br>• An activity<br>• A unit | •<br>•<br>•<br>•<br>•<br>•<br>•<br>• |

## Independent Write

Students work independently to outline a chapter. If students are unfamiliar with outlining, some instruction will be necessary. Younger students may work in pairs to outline the text.

## RoundTable

When students are done creating their outlines, they join teammates. Each teammate has an outline of the text. The team's task is to create a summary of the text, using only their outlines. Student One suggests the first sentence of the summary by saying it aloud. If teammates agree, he or she writes it down, then passes the paper and pen to the next teammate to write the next summary sentence. If a student requests help, teammates can help come up with the sentence. This process continues until students have written a summary of the text or chapter.

Virginia DeBolt: *Write! Science*
Kagan Cooperative Learning • 1 (800) WEE CO-OP

# Outline Review

**Name** _____ **Date** _____

**Directions:** Fill in your topic of review in the box below. Using only your outlines, write a summary of the text chapter. Take turns writing each sentence. Ask for help if you need it.

*Summary of* _____
                                    *review topic*

Virginia DeBolt: *Write! Science*
Kagan Cooperative Learning • 1 (800) WEE CO-OP

# Science Jeopardy

Everyone loves the quiz show Jeopardy. In this activity, students play Science Jeopardy in their teams. Students write questions reviewing science topics covered and the answers to their questions. In teams, they take turns quizzing each other.

## ACTIVITY 28 at-a-glance

**Cooperative Structure**
- RoundRobin

**Level of Thinking**
- Application

**Multiple Intelligences**
- Verbal/Linguistic
- Interpersonal

### Idea Bank

| Ideas for my class... | More ideas for my class... |
|---|---|
| **Play Jeopardy with:**<br>• Review topics<br>• Vocabulary words<br>• Formulas | •<br>•<br>•<br>•<br>•<br>•<br>•<br>•<br>•<br>• |

## Independent Write

Students use their texts or notes to write as many review questions as they can as well as the answers to their questions on the reproducible.

## RoundRobin

After students have a number of review questions and answers, students review with teammates. In turn, students read an answer to the team. For example "Head, thorax and abdomen." The first teammate to raise his or her hand gets to provide the question, "What are the three body parts of an insect?"

Students can play for points. A less competitive alternative is to have the student to the left get the first opportunity to provide the question to the answer. This can also be done on flashcards to send problems to other teams to answer. Jeopardy can also be played as a class, with teams competing against each other.

Virginia DeBolt: *Write! Science*
Kagan Cooperative Learning • 1 (800) WEE CO-OP

# Science Jeopardy

Name _____ Date _____

**Directions:** Fill in the review topic in the box below. Write as many review questions and answers as you can. See if you can stump your teammates.

_____ Jeopardy
          topic

A _____
  _____
Q _____
  _____

A _____
  _____
Q _____
  _____

A _____
  _____
Q _____
  _____

A _____
  _____
Q _____
  _____

A _____
  _____
Q _____
  _____

Virginia DeBolt: *Write! Science*
Kagan Cooperative Learning • 1 (800) WEE CO-OP

# What I Learned

After learning about a topic, it is helpful to have students reflect on what they learned. Reflection helps students process and assimilate new information. In this activity, students work in pairs to list what they learned about the topic. Students, then write a paper reviewing what they learned.

## ACTIVITY 29

at-a-glance

**Cooperative Structures**
- RallyTable
- RoundRobin

**Level of Thinking**
- Analysis
- Synthesis

**Multiple Intelligences**
- Verbal/Linguistic
- Logical/Mathematical
- Interpersonal
- Intrapersonal

### IDEA BANK

*Ideas for my class...*

What I learned about the:
- Lesson
- Chapter
- Unit
- Presentation
- Experiment
- Video

*More ideas for my class...*

## RallyTable
In pairs, students take turns writing down all the information they covered in the lesson chapter, or unit, or what they learned from a presentation, film, video or experiment. Students say what they learned to their partner before they write it down.

## Independent Write
After pairs have listed everything that they can remember about what they learned, partners separate and each student writes his or her own summary of what he or she learned. Students can also write how they feel about the topic.

## RoundRobin
In turn, students read their What I Learned papers to teammates.

Virginia DeBolt: *Write! Science*
Kagan Cooperative Learning • 1 (800) WEE CO-OP

# What I Learned

**Name** _____ **Date** _____

**Directions:** Fill in the learning topic in the blank below. Write about what you learned and how you feel about the topic.

What I learned about _____.
                              *topic*

_____
_____
_____
_____
_____
_____
_____
_____
_____
_____
_____
_____
_____
_____
_____
_____
_____
_____
_____
_____

Virginia DeBolt: *Write! Science*
Kagan Cooperative Learning • 1 (800) WEE CO-OP

# Some Interesting Consequences

*Science is full of causal relationships. If bobcats die, deer multiply, deer eat the ground cover causing mice and rabbits to starve. With fewer mice and rabbits, raptors starve too. In this activity, students explore the consequences of different actions, draw a diagram and write about the consequences.*

## ACTIVITY 30

### at-a-glance

**Cooperative Structures**
- Think-Pair-Share
- Pair Project
- RoundRobin

**Level of Thinking**
- Application
- Analysis

**Multiple Intelligences**
- Verbal/Linguistic
- Visual/Spatial
- Interpersonal
- Naturalist

### IDEA BANK

| Ideas for my class... | More ideas for my class... |
|---|---|
| **What are the consequences of:** | • |
| • Polar ice melts | • |
| • Bobcats die of disease | • |
| • Earth's magnetic pole shifts | • |
| • Petroleum found on Venus | • |
| • Global warming | • |
| • Cold fusion | • |
| • Sharks extinct | • |

## Think-Pair-Share

Present a problem to the class with interesting consequences. A food chain example: "What might happen if all the bobcats suddenly died?" Give students a good 10-15 seconds of think time. "Pair up and tell your partner what you predict would happen." Give students 30–60 seconds to discuss the consequences. Pick a few students to share their ideas with the class. For example, a student might suggest that prey normally consumed by bobcats would increase in greater than usual numbers. "Think about this without talking—if deer populations grew due to the absence of bobcats, what would happen next?" Continue probing students and having them discuss in pairs until you feel the students have explored all the implications for the food chain.

Virginia DeBolt: *Write! Science*
Kagan Cooperative Learning • 1 (800) WEE CO-OP

# Some Interesting Consequences

### ACTIVITY 30

## Pair Project
Have students work with their partner to diagram all the consequences they discussed as well as they heard from other students. See sample consequence diagram below.

## Independent Write
After students create a detailed diagram, they are to work independently to write a paper on the consequences of the action. Students can refer to their diagrams as they wirte

## RoundRobin
Students take turns reading their paper to the team.

*Sample consequence diagram*

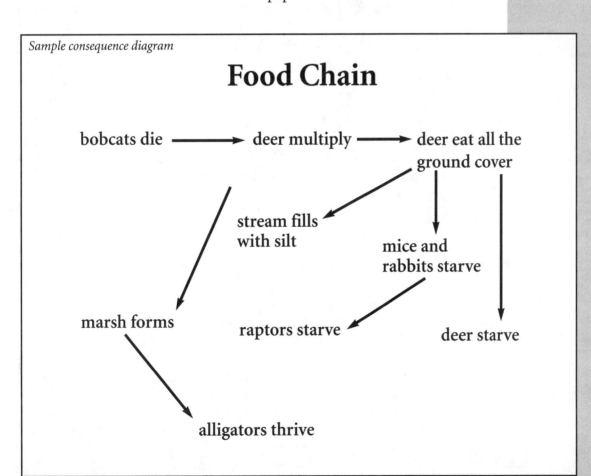

Virginia DeBolt: *Write! Science*
Kagan Cooperative Learning • 1 (800) WEE CO-OP

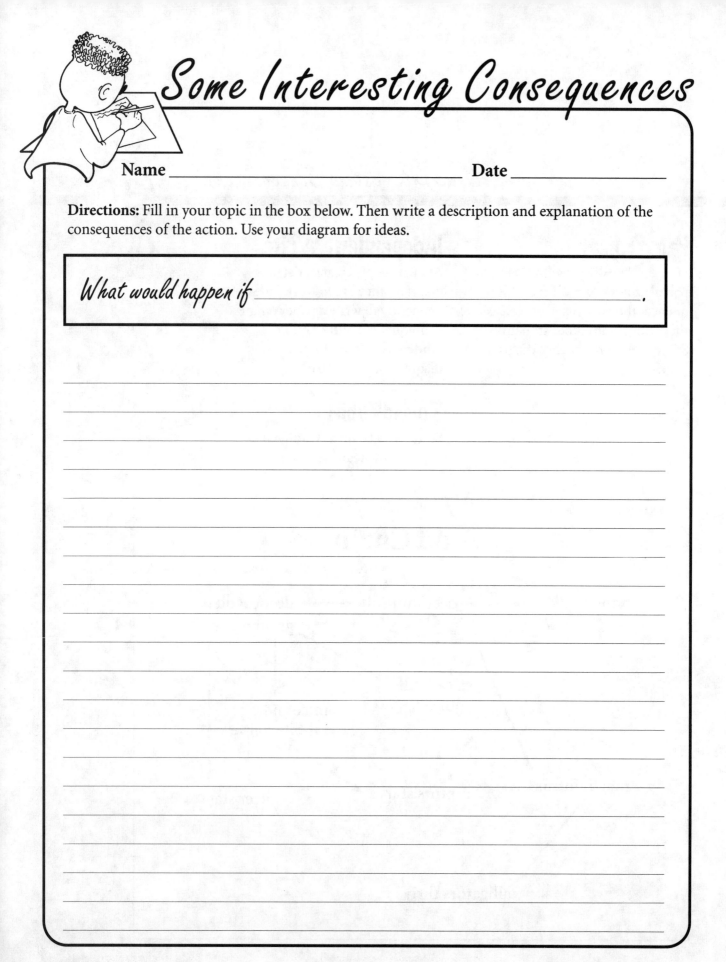

# Journal Topics

- Some species of insects have a life span of only a few hours. What do you think they do during that time?

- What should be done with all the plutonium from dismantled nuclear weapons?

- How would you explain the carbon-oxygen cycle to someone?

- What science experiment would you enjoy doing again? Why?

- Write about a science report you heard or read in the news this week.

# Experiment Reflections

Experimentation is one of a scientists greatest tools for discovering truths about the world. Often times, experiments generate more questions than they answer. In this activity, students reflect on the purpose, procedure and findings of their experiment and think about the implications of the research for new areas of inquiry.

## ACTIVITY 31 at-a-glance

**Cooperative Structure**
• Think-Pair-Write

**Level of Thinking**
• Synthesis
• Evaluation

**Multiple Intelligences**
• Verbal/Linguistic
• Logical/Mathematical
• Interpersonal

### IDEA BANK

| Ideas for my class... | More ideas for my class... |
|---|---|
| • Use this activity to reflect on any experiment | • <br> • <br> • <br> • <br> • <br> • <br> • <br> • <br> • |

## Think-Pair-Write

Students reflect on their experiments and implications for more research using the questions on the reproducible as prompts. Ask the first question, "What was the purpose of your experiment?" Give students 10-15 seconds of think time. Then, students pair to discuss their ideas. Let them discuss the prompt for 45 seconds to a minute. Students write their own idea, their partner's idea, a combination of both ideas, or some new idea which grew from the pair discussion.

The steps are then repeated for every question on the reproducible.

This activity can also be done independently, then shared with teammates or together as a team, each student taking turns recording each team answer.

Virginia DeBolt: *Write! Science*
Kagan Cooperative Learning • 1 (800) WEE CO-OP

# Experiment Reflections

**Name** _____ **Date** _____

**Directions:** Fill in the topic of your experiment in the box below. Answer the following question on your experiment.

| Reflections on _____ . |
|---|
| experiment topic |

What was the purpose of your experiment? _____
_____
_____

Summarize the procedure of the experiment. _____
_____
_____
_____

What were the findings of your experiment? _____
_____
_____
_____

State your results as a theory. _____
_____
_____
_____

What are some questions you have about the topic? _____
_____
_____

What experiment could you perform to test your theory or answer your questions? ___
_____
_____

*Virginia DeBolt: Write! Science*
Kagan Cooperative Learning • 1 (800) WEE CO-OP

# Singing Science

An amazing amount of information can be contained in a song. Here is the opportunity for some of your musically-inclined students to apply their music smarts to learn about science. In this activity, pairs research and write a song to a familiar tune. Pairs sing their science as a duet to the class.

## ACTIVITY 32 at-a-glance

### Cooperative Structures

- Pair Project
- Simultaneous Chalkboard Share
- Pairs Present

### Level of Thinking

- Application
- Synthesis

### Multiple Intelligences

- Verbal/Linguistic
- Musical/Rhythmic
- Interpersonal

## IDEA BANK

| Ideas for my class... | More ideas for my class... |
|---|---|
| **Write a song about:**<br>• Famous scientists<br>• Plant<br>• Animal<br>• Physics<br>• Chemistry<br>• Biology<br>• Oceanography<br>• Geology<br>• Astronomy<br>• Inventors | •<br>•<br>•<br>•<br>•<br>•<br>•<br>•<br>•<br>• |

## Pair Project

Students pair up to research their science topic and to compose a song about their topic using a familiar tune. Some familiar tunes students can use include: *Jingle Bells, Old MacDonald, Mary Had a Little Lamb, When the Saints Go Marching In, My Bonnie Lies Over the Ocean, Rudolph the Red-Nosed Reindeer.*

## Simultaneous Chalkboard Share

When pairs have completed their songs, they go to a designated area of the chalkboard and write the lyrics of their song large enough for the whole class to see.

## Pairs Present

Pairs take turns singing their science song to the class. Alternatively, pairs can share their songs with other pairs.

Virginia DeBolt: *Write! Science*

# Singing Science

**Name** _____  **Date** _____

**Directions:** Fill in the topic of your science song in the box below. Write your song to a familiar tune. Don't forget to include all relevant facts about your topic. Be prepared to share your song with the class.

*Our science song on* _____ .
                                        *topic*

# Creature Creation

Asking students to create a new, original creature gives them a chance to have fun while using everything they know about biology, zoology and ecology. In this activity, students write about a new creature, then share it with teammates.

## ACTIVITY 33 at-a-glance

| Ideas for my class... | More ideas for my class... |
|---|---|
| **Use this activity when learning about:**<br>• Body systems<br>• Animal kingdom<br>• Adaptations | •<br>•<br>•<br>•<br>•<br>•<br>•<br>•<br>•<br>• |

**IDEA BANK**

### Cooperative Structure
• RoundRobin

### Level of Thinking
• Application
• Analysis
• Synthesis

### Multiple Intelligences
• Verbal/Linguistic
• Interpersonal
• Naturalist

## Independent Write

Tell students that they have discovered a new creature, previously unknown to mankind. Their jobs as the discoverer of this new creature is to introduce it to the world. They must describe how the creature looks, what it eats, where it lives, who its natural enemies are, and its particular characteristics. To do this, students answer the questions on the reproducible. When done describing their creatures, students draw their creatures on a separate sheet of paper.

## RoundRobin

Students share what they wrote about their creature with teammates, then share their drawing of their creature.

Students will be interested in reading about each other's creatures. Creature drawings and descriptions can be posted in a "creative museum" or on a bulletin board.

Virginia DeBolt: *Write! Science*
Kagan Cooperative Learning • 1 (800) WEE CO-OP

# Creature Creation

Name _____ Date _____

**Directions:** Fill in the name of your creature in the box below. Create a new creature. Answer the following questions about your creature. When done, draw a picture of your creature on a separate sheet of paper.

| My creature's name _____ . |

What does your creature look like? Describe it as well as possible. _____
_____
_____
_____
_____

What does your creature eat? _____
_____
_____
_____
_____

Where does your creature live? _____
_____
_____
_____
_____

Who are your creature's natural enemies? _____
_____
_____
_____
_____

Virginia DeBolt: *Write! Science*
Kagan Cooperative Learning • 1 (800) WEE CO-OP

# Analyze Cause and Effect

If you dump motor oil on the ground, then you pollute your drinking water. If every inch of an urban area is paved, then human behavior is affected. If birds are plentiful, then insect population is reduced. In this activity, pairs investigate the scientific causes of a given effect and make a poster illustrating the cause-effect relationships. Pairs share their posters with another pair and students independently write about the cause-effect relationship of the topic of investigation.

## ACTIVITY 34
### at-a-glance

**Cooperative Structures**
- Pair Project
- Pairs Present

**Level of Thinking**
- Analysis

**Multiple Intelligences**
- Verbal/Linguistic
- Logical/Mathematical
- Visual/Spatial
- Interpersonal

### IDEA BANK

| Ideas for my class... | More ideas for my class... |
|---|---|
| **What is the cause of:**<br>• Greenhouse effect<br>• Red tide<br>• Rainbows<br>• Lung disease<br>• Soil depletion<br>• Oak tree blight<br>• Ozone alert days<br>• Unsafe drinking water<br>• Endangered species status<br>• Blue sky | •<br>•<br>•<br>•<br>•<br>•<br>•<br>•<br>•<br>• |

## Pair Project
Assign pairs a topic that has a scientific cause or many causes. For example, it is known that lung cancer is *caused* by cigarette smoking. If you are studying an effect that has multiple causes, consider assigning different causes to each group. Partners work together to investigate the cause or causes for their assigned effect. Pairs make a poster illustrating the cause(s) of the topic of research.

## Pairs Present
Pairs present their poster to another pair. Following each presentation, the listening pair offers praise and asks any questions.

## Independent Write
After students have investigated and shared their learning with others, have them write a summary of what they learned about cause and effect relationship.

# Analyze Cause and Effect

Name _____ Date _____

**Directions:** Fill in the effect you investigated in the box below. Write a description of the cause(s) for the effect. If the effect is undesirable, how might changes come about?

The causes for _____.
                                    *effect*

Virginia DeBolt: *Write! Science*
Kagan Cooperative Learning • 1 (800) WEE CO-OP

# My Opinion

Many scientific pursuits have associated ethical issues. Cloning has been demonstrated with animals, should we clone humans? Students need to form reasoned opinions based on fact. In this activity, students explore ethical issues and write on their opinions.

## ACTIVITY 35 at-a-glance

### Materials Needed
- Curriculum materials, current periodicals & scientific journals about the topics in question

### Cooperative Structures
- Agreement Circles
- RoundRobin

### Level of Thinking
- Analysis
- Evaluation

### Multiple Intelligences
- Verbal/Linguistic
- Interpersonal
- Intrapersonal

### Ideas for my class...
**What's your opinion on:**
- Gene manipulation
- Teaching birth control information in public school
- Testing beauty products on animals
- Experimentation with human subjects

### More ideas for my class...
- 
- 
- 
- 
- 
- 
- 

### IDEA BANK

## Agreement Circles

Have the class stand in a large circle in open space in the classroom. Stand in the middle of the circle and make a statement on an ethical issue that students can respond in varying degrees of agreement or disagreement. For example, you might state, "It makes good sense to transplant baboon hearts into humans with bad hearts."

After hearing the statement, students decide whether they agree or disagree. Students who strongly disagree with your statement will not move from the perimeter of the circle. Students who strongly agree with your statement will move to the center of the circle, very close to you. Students who agree somewhat or see both sides of the issue, will walk about half way into the center of the circle. After students have taken their new positions, pair them in these ways:

- "Pair with someone near you who agrees with your position. Talk about your opinion on the statement."
- "Pair with someone farther away from you who disagrees with your position. Talk about your opinion on the statement."

Virginia DeBolt: *Write! Science*
Kagan Cooperative Learning • 1 (800) WEE CO-OP

# My Opinion

ACTIVITY 35

- "Pair with someone who sees both sides of the issue. Talk about your opinion on the statement."

## Independent Write

After the discussion, have students return to their desks. They have discussed their idea in several ways. In addition, students have heard the arguments of those who disagree with them. Since students know what the objections to their position may be, supporting ideas aimed at refuting those objections should be among the ideas advanced in the writing.

Tell students that they will write a persuasive letter to the President, stating their opinion on the issue. An effective format for the letters:

**Paragraph 1:** State topic and main idea or position.

**Paragraphs 2-4:** Write separate, detailed paragraphs for each of the three supporting facts.

**Paragraph 5:** Conclude with strongest point and restate opinion.

## RoundRobin

Students share their persuasive opinion papers in turn with teammates. Teammates can paraphrase and give feedback.

Virginia DeBolt: *Write! Science*
Kagan Cooperative Learning • 1 (800) WEE CO-OP

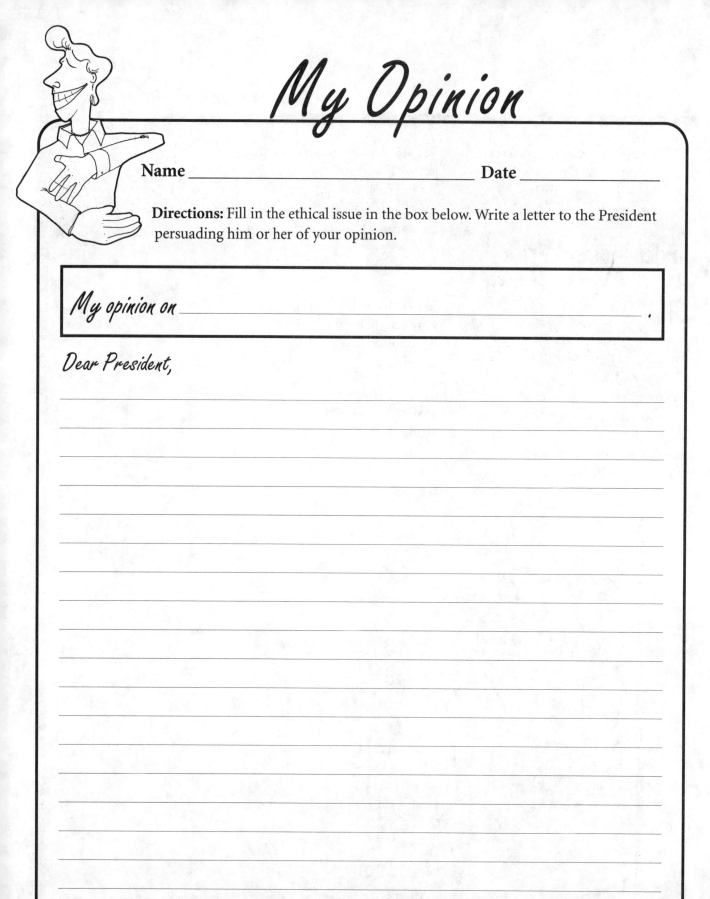

# Journal Topics

- Write a one sentence summary of each section in the chapter.

- Write a one sentence summary of the results of an experiment.

- Write riddles for which the answer is a vocabulary word.

- Predict ten-year changes in the topic covered in the chapter.

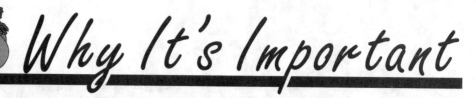

# Why It's Important

Have you ever heard students ask, "Why do we need to learn this?" or exclaim, "I don't care about this!" Without seeing the relevance or importance of an issue, students may see it as just something to learn for the test. In this activity, students explore and write about the importance or personal relevance of the issue at hand.

## ACTIVITY 36 at-a-glance

**Cooperative Structure**
- Mix-Freeze-Pair

**Level of Thinking**
- Application
- Analysis

**Multiple Intelligences**
- Verbal/Linguistic
- Logical/Mathematical
- Interpersonal
- Intrapersonal

### IDEA BANK

| Ideas for my class... | More ideas for my class... |
|---|---|
| • Use this activity to explore the importance of any topic of study | • <br> • <br> • <br> • <br> • <br> • <br> • <br> • |

## Mix-Freeze-Pair

With note pad in hand, students get out of their seats and "Mix" about the classroom. They continue to circulate aimlessly until you call, "Freeze." Ask the class why the topic is important and how they relate it personally. For example, "Why is studying the structure of a cell important? How does it relate to you?" Students then pair with the closest person and discuss for 30 seconds about why the topic is important. Students can take notes. Say "Mix," and students again wander until you call "Freeze," and "Pair" for another round of discussion. Repeat these steps a number of times until students have paired with several individuals.

## Independent Write

Have the students write a list of the top ten reasons to learn about the topic.

Virginia DeBolt: *Write! Science*
Kagan Cooperative Learning • 1 (800) WEE CO-OP

# Why It's Important

Why?

Name _____ Date _____

**Directions:** Fill in the topic in the blank below. Write the top 10 reasons the topic is important to learn about.

Why is _____ important?
*topic*

1. _____
2. _____
3. _____
4. _____
5. _____
6. _____
7. _____
8. _____
9. _____
10. _____

Virginia DeBolt: *Write! Science*
Kagan Cooperative Learning • 1 (800) WEE CO-OP

# Part III: Cooperative Learning Structures

The directions regarding the structures used in the writing activities were specific for that activity. In this section of the book, you will find a more general description of the structures, one which may help you see how you can apply it in other ways in your classroom.

Dr. Spencer Kagan's book *Cooperative Learning* is the definitive resource and guide to cooperative learning structures. He has designed and refined over one hundred cooperative learning strategies, each one carefully planned to include the principles of cooperative learning. Those principles are:

- **Positive Interdependence**
- **Individual Accountability**
- **Equal Participation**
- **Simultaneous Interaction**

Using cooperative learning structures helps you achieve success with cooperative learning because the basic principles to successful cooperative learning are "built in." The marvelous thing about the structures is that they are content free. If you use an activity from this book involving Think-Pair-Share or RoundRobin with writing content, you can use these cooperative structures equally well with any content. From kindergarten to graduate school, from astrophysics to plumbing repair, cooperative learning structures are helpful tools to build effective learning experiences.

### Structure 1

# Agreement Circles

*Students demonstrate their agreement or disagreement with an issue by physically locating themselves in the Agreement Circle. Agreement Circles is a great way to have students explore their own values as well as those of classmates.*

Tell students to form a large circle in open space in the classroom. Stand in the middle of the circle and make a value statement. The statement must be worded so that students can respond with a measure of agreement or disagreement. Sample statements: "The needs of a tiny, obscure species should not be placed ahead of the needs of thousands of people." Or, "It makes good sense to transplant baboon hearts into humans with bad hearts." After hearing the statement, students decide whether or not they agree with the statement. Students who strongly disagree with your statement do not move from the perimeter of the circle. Students who strongly agree with your statement move to the center of the circle, near you. Students who disagree somewhat or see both sides of the issue, step into the center of the circle in proportion to their agreement.

After students have taken their new positions in the Agreement Circle, pair them in these ways:
- "Pair with someone near you who agrees with your position. Talk about your opinion on the statement."
- "Pair with someone away from you who disagrees with your position. Talk about your opinion on the statement."
- "Pair with someone who sees both sides of the issue. Talk about your opinion on the statement."

Students can develop their own value statements on the issue and take turns leading Agreement Circles.

Virginia DeBolt: *Write! Science*
Kagan Cooperative Learning • 1 (800) WEE CO-OP

# Corners

***Students chose between the alternatives posted in the corners of the classroom, and share the rationale for their choices with students with similar and different choices. Corners is a great way to promote participation, discussion and to have students hear multiple perspectives.***

Come up with four alternatives from which to choose from relating to the lesson. Try to select alternatives that will divide the class about equally into fours. A science related example: "Would you rather be a: 1) Marine Biologist, 2) Surgeon, 3) Astronomer, or 4) Geologist?" Post the alternatives in the four corners of the classroom. Give students time to think about their preference, then have them write down their choice on a slip of paper. (Having students write down their corner of choice reduces the likelihood of students selecting a corner because someone else did.) Tell students to go to the corner they selected. While in their corners, have students form pairs or groups of four to discuss the topic or to work on the content involved in the lesson. Select some students from each corner to share with the class why they selected their corner.

Virginia DeBolt: *Write! Science*

## Structure 3

# 4S Brainstorming

*Students each fulfill a role as they quickly brainstorm ideas as a team. 4S Brainstorming is an effective way to generate a range of creative ideas.*

In teams of four, each student is assigned a role for the brainstorming session:
- **Speed Captain** - Applies time pressure. Creativity increases with speed.
- **Sergeant Support** - Encourages all ideas. Students contribute more when ideas are praised.
- **Sultan of Silly** - Encourages silly ideas and off-the-wall thinking. Promotes creative ideas.
- **Synergy Guru** - Encourages building on ideas.

One student can record all the team's ideas or students can take turns recording each new idea.

## Structure 4

# Mix-Freeze-Pair

*Students "Mix" in the classroom, "Freeze" in place, then form "Pairs" to discuss the topic presented by the teacher. Mix-Freeze-Pair provides students a fun and energizing format to share their ideas and hear the ideas of classmates in randomly formed discussion pairs.*

Students get out of their seats and circulate freely through the classroom. When you call, "Freeze," students freeze in their tracks. Announce the discussion topic. For example, "How could we promote recycling at our school?" Then call, "Pair." Students pair up with their closest classmate to discuss the topic. After pairs thoroughly discuss the topic, repeat the process. As a rule, students can not pair with the same partner twice. With each new pairing, students hear a fresh perspective on the same topic or can discuss another topic presented by the teacher.

Cooperative Learning Structures

### Structure 5

# Pair Discussion

*Students pair up to discuss any topic. Pair Discussion provides an intimate setting that promotes active discussion and listening.*

Pair Discussion is simply two students pairing up for a brief time during which they discuss the matter under study. They might discuss the best way to do something, the best answer to a question, the steps in a process, or the meaning of a vocabulary word.

### Structure 6

# Pair Project

*Students work together with a partner to complete a project. Pairs provide students the opportunity to collaborate efforts, yet are small enough to maximize participation.*

In Pair Project, two students pair up to work on an assigned project. The project can involve any type of pair work: creating products, doing research, solving problems, conducting experiments, inventing new machines. It is a good idea to create a project that neither student could do alone or to structure the project so that both students must contribute. This way, students are both accountable for their contribution and no one student can do all the work.

Virginia DeBolt: *Write! Science*

*Structure 7*

# Pairs Check

*In a series of simple steps, students work together to master any content. Pairs Check is an excellent way to provide students with immediate tutoring and feedback.*

Pairs Check involves eight simple steps:

**Step 1. Pair Work.** Teams break into two sets of pairs. Partners work on a single set of questions or problems. One student works on the first problem while the other watches and coaches, helping if necessary.

**Step 2. Coach Checks.** The coach checks his or her partner's work for agreement. If the partners don't agree on an answer, they may ask the other pair on the team.

**Step 3. Coach Praises.** If the partners agree, the coach offers a praiser.

**Steps 4-6. Partners Switch Roles.** The partners switch roles and repeat steps 1-3.

**Step 7. Pairs Check.** The two pairs on the team get together to check their answers. If they disagree and are unable to figure out why, four hands go up.

**Step 8. Team Celebrates.** If the team agrees on the answer, they congratulate each other.

1. Pair Work   2. Coach Checks   3. Coach Praises
4. Pair Work   5. Coach Checks   6. Coach Praises
7. Pairs Check   8. Teams Celebrate

Virginia DeBolt: *Write! Science*
Kagan Cooperative Learning • 1 (800) WEE CO-OP

Cooperative Learning Structures

**Structure 8**

# Pairs Present

*Pairs present their project with another pair, team, or the class. Pairs Present is an excellent way for students to share information with classmates and hone their presentation skills.*

When two students have worked together on a project, assignment or experiment and have a product or results to share with the class, use Pairs Present. The two should participate equally in the presentation, and in some way be held individually accountable for knowing all the information involved in the assignment.

**Structure 9**

# RallyTable

*In pairs, students take turns writing. RallyTable is a quick and easy way to generate and record ideas or write pair papers. The turn-taking ensures equal participation.*

RallyTable is the pair alternative to RoundTable. Pairs share a common piece of paper, which they hand back and forth, each contributing in turn. Science examples to use Rallytable might be: "Come up with a list of everything you know about spiders, taking turns writing each fact." Or, "Write a paragraph on what you know about spiders, taking turns writing each sentence."

Cooperative Learning Structures

*Structure 10*

# RoundRobin

***Each student, in turn, shares with teammates. Roundrobin is an easy way to have students share any information with teammates in a format that ensures equal participation.***

RoundRobin is simply speaking in turn within teams. For example, students can share how they feel about space exploration or can read their papers on space exploration to teammates. Many conditions can be attached to RoundRobin to make it achieve the results desired. For example, each person must speak for thirty seconds and no longer; or each person must quickly paraphrase (or praise) the previous person's comments before making their own; or each person must offer something new to the RoundRobin.

*Structure 11*

# RoundTable

***In teams, students take turns writing. Roundtable is a great way to generate a list of ideas or to write team papers. The turn-taking ensures equal participation.***

RoundTable is a written RoundRobin. Ideas, answers, or any type of contribution is made as the paper is passed around the table. RoundTable is an excellent structure for brainstorming and generating lists, especially if it is done quickly. For example, "List as many elements as you can." RoundTable also works well for writing as a team. Each student must participate in the team writing task. For example, "Write a brief description of the Periodic Table. Take turns writing each sentence."

Virginia DeBolt: *Write! Science*
Kagan Cooperative Learning • 1 (800) WEE CO-OP

Cooperative Learning Structures

Structure 12

# Send-A-Problem

*Students generate questions and send them to other teams to solve. Send-A-Problem is an effective way to review learning materials and practice team problem-solving skills.*

Each student writes a question or problem on a card. For review, have students write high-consensus questions for which there is a clear correct answer. Send-A-Problem can also be used with higher-level thinking questions that promote team discussion on the topic. Students check their questions or problems with teammates. If there is total consensus, the answer is written on the back of the card. (No answer is needed for higher-level thinking questions as there is usually no right or wrong answer.) Questions can also be written together as a team on a sheet of paper with the answers on the back or on a separate answer key. When teams have completed their questions or problems, they send them to another team to solve.

Student One reads the first problem aloud to teammates. The team works together to answer the problem. Problems can also be solved in pairs. Students check their answers by flipping over the card or checking with the key. If the team disagrees with the answer, they can work with the sending team to solve the discrepancy. Student Two reads the next card and the process is repeated until all the problems have been read and answered.

After the team has solved all problems or after a determined amount of time has passed, teams send the problems to another team to answer.

Virginia DeBolt: *Write! Science*
Kagan Cooperative Learning • 1 (800) WEE CO-OP

*Structure 13*

# Simultaneous Chalkboard Share

*A representative from each team simultaneously records the team's answer or idea on the chalkboard to share with the class. Simultaneous Chalkboard Share promotes information sharing among teams while saving valuable time.*

Just as students benefit from sharing questions, answers and ideas within teams, teams can benefit by sharing with other teams. Teams can build on each other's ideas; an idea shared may trigger a whole new direction for exploration or spark new ideas for discussion. A representative from each team simultaneously records the team's answer or idea on a designated area of the chalkboard. Representatives can be team selected, or you can select each team's representative by announcing a student number, "Student Threes, please record your team's answer on the chalkboard." In a brief amount of time and with little interruption to the teamwork, all teams have access to each other's ideas or answers.

*Structure 14*

# Simultaneous RoundTable

*In teams, students simultaneously write down an idea, then pass the paper for a teammate to record the next idea. In Simultaneous RoundTable, all students are actively participating as they simultaneously make contributions to the team's paper.*

In Simultaneous RoundTable, each teammates pulls out a sheet of paper. They each record the first idea or sentence to the paper, then pass the paper clockwise. Teammates read the information on the paper, make a contribution, then pass it clockwise again. When completed, each team has four papers loaded with ideas or four different writings on a topic or on different, related topics. Simultaneous RoundTable can also be used to edit each other's work. Often, a set length of time is determined by the teacher. Students pass papers when you call, "Pass."

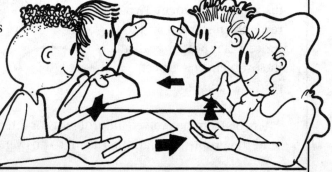

Virginia DeBolt: *Write! Science*
Kagan Cooperative Learning • 1 (800) WEE CO-OP

## Structure 15

# Team Discussion

*Students discuss any topic as a team. Team Discussion is a simple, unstructured platform for students to share their ideas with teammates.*

The teacher announces the topic to discuss. Discussion topics are usually open-ended with no right or wrong answers. For example, "How did you feel about dissecting the earthworm?" Following the Team Discussion, select one student from several teams share their ideas with the entire class.

## Structure 16

# Team Interview

*Students on each team are interviewed, in turn, by teammates. Team Interview is a great way for students to share with teammates and to probe teammates for information.*

In Team Interview, one student on the team is selected to go first. He or she stands up. Teammates have a predetermined amount of time to ask him or her questions to learn as much as they can about the topic. When the time is up, the next student stands, and teammates pump him or her for information.

A simple variation is to have students present information to teammates first, then teammates may ask additional questions.

### Structure 17

# Team Project

*Students work together as a team to complete a team project. Team Projects provide students a great deal of autonomy as they work cooperatively toward a common goal.*

The teacher announces the team project. Each team may have a unique project or all teams may work on the same project. Projects can involve any type of teamwork: creating products, doing research, solving problems, composing a song, conducting experiments, coordinating a dance or movement. Without any structure, students may run into complications with a project. One or two students may do all of the work while the others do not contribute at all. To avoid this pitfall, try one or more of the following ideas:

• **Assign Roles** - Assign each student a role specific to the project. As a class, brainstorm and have students record "Things to Do" and "Things to Say" to fulfill each role. Some generic roles you may use include: Checker, Cheerleader, Coach, Encourager, Gatekeeper, Materials Monitor, Praiser, Question Commander, Quiet Captain, Recorder, Reflector, Taskmaster.

• **Divide the Work** - Divide the work of the project or have students divide the work so that everyone must participate.

• **Limit the Resources** - By limiting who can use which resources, students depend on each other for completing the project.

• **Individual Papers or Tests** - Have students each turn in their own paper on the topic or be responsible for their own learning. Do not use group grades for team projects.

# Team Sort

*Students work as a team to sort items or information into a predetermined system. Team Sort develops classification, categorization and sorting skills.*

Working together as a team, students sort items into given categories or into a categorization system like a Venn diagram, two-by-two matrix, or a ranking ladder. The items for sorting can be generated by a team brainstorming session or can be provided. Students take turns placing items into the categorization system. When teams are done sorting, they can share or compare their resulting product with another team, or post their work for the class to see.

In Team Sort, also called Structured Sort, the categorization system is provided; in Unstructured Sort, students make up their own categorization systems.

**Sample categorization systems:**

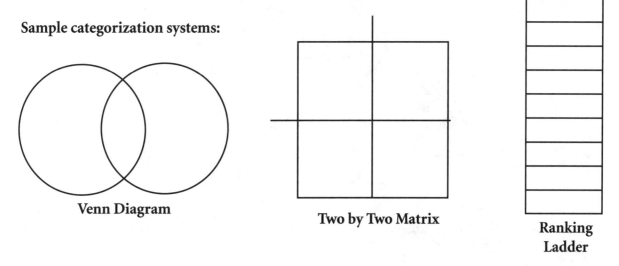

Venn Diagram     Two by Two Matrix     Ranking Ladder

## Structure 19

# Teams Present

*Teams share their project with another team or with the class. Teams Present is a great way to practice presentation skills and disseminate information.*

Following an activity or project in which the teams have worked to make a product or demonstrate an idea, have them present their work to another team or to the class. Presenting to one other team has the advantage of more active participation and a distinct time advantage. For each team to do a five-minute presentation to the class, with eight teams would take about 40 minutes. Of the 40 minutes, students are active presenters for five minutes and passive viewers for 35 minutes. Teams can present to one other team and watch one other team's five-minute presentation in just 10 minutes, all of which they are active presenters or viewers. In the same amount of time as a class presentation, teams can share their presentation and view one other team's presentation four times. Repeated practice allows students the opportunity to hone their presentation skills. Presenting to the whole class has the advantage of a larger audience and the advantage of every student getting the opportunity to see every team's presentation.

Regardless of whether students present to one other team, to several teams, or to the whole class, it is still important to make sure each student is individually accountable for his or her own contribution. Students can be held accountable by each presenting part of the information, turning in a paper on the presentation, or being held responsible for all material in the presentation.

# Team Word Web

*Students work in teams to create a web of ideas and details on a given topic. Word Webs promote divergent thinking and visually depict the interrelations of the learning material.*

To make word webs in teams, give each student a different colored marker and each team a large sheet of butcher paper. Word webs can also be made on smaller paper. The main topic of the word web is written in a rectangle in the center of the paper. Students do a RoundTable, adding core concepts sprouting from the main topics, circling the core concepts in the ovals. Then, students have a free-for-all, adding as many supporting details as possible and making connections where appropriate. Encourage students to suspend judgment and to quickly write down and integrate everything that comes to mind.

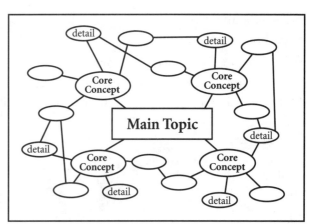

Have students add illustrations, symbols, bridges, and graphics to make mind maps.

Virginia DeBolt: *Write! Science*

*Structure 21*

# ThinkPad Brainstorming

*Students generate a number of ideas on a given topic, each on a separate thinkpad slip and share their ideas with teammates. ThinkPad Brainstorming promotes creative thinking.*

In ThinkPad Brainstorming, students work individually, recording their brainstormed ideas on thinkpad slips, small sheets of paper or cards. After a period of time or after students have generated enough ideas on a topic, students share their ideas in a RoundRobin. Teammates work together to see if they can build on ideas generated or come up with new and even better ideas. The ideas that are generated can be easily sorted and categorized. See Team Sort.

# Think-Pair-Share

**Structure 22**

*After a question or topic is announced by the teacher, students "Think" about the question, "Pair" up with a partner to discuss the question, then some students are selected to "Share" their ideas with the class. Think-Pair-Share is a simple and powerful technique for developing and sharing ideas.*

The teacher poses a question for the class to think about. Think-Pair-Share works best with low-consensus, thinking questions to which there is not a right or wrong answer. For example, some questions to spark some interest on endangered species, "Some species are threatened with extinction. Should we let natural selection run its course, or should we intervene?" Or, "What are some things we could do to help protect the bald eagle?" Give students a good 10-15 seconds of think time. Then, have students pair up with another student on their team to share what they think. After students have shared their ideas, select a few students to share with the class their ideas, or their partner's ideas. Think-Pair-Share can be used several times in succession to follow a line of reasoning or more fully develop a concept with interrelated issues. Have students pair up with a different teammate with each new question.

1. Think
2. Pair
3. Share

Virginia DeBolt: *Write! Science*
Kagan Cooperative Learning • 1 (800) WEE CO-OP

## Structure 23

# Think-Pair-Write

*In this variation of Think-Pair-Share, instead of selecting a few students to share their ideas with the class after the think and pair discussion time, have all students write down their ideas. Think-Pair-Write is an excellent way to prime the writing pump.*

Think-Pair-Write substitutes a writing component for Think-Pair-Share's last step, sharing with the class. After the think time and pair discussion, students write down their own ideas, the ideas their partner shared, or even new ideas. Students can do a number of Think-Pair-Writes in succession to discuss and develop ideas on the topic. For a fresh perspective on the same topic, repeat the question and have students pair with a new teammate. Think-Pair-Write is a great way to pique students' interest in a topic and is an excellent prewriting activity. After several rounds of Think-Pair-Write, students will have discussed the topic in detail and developed a set of notes which they may use for the basis of writing on the topic.

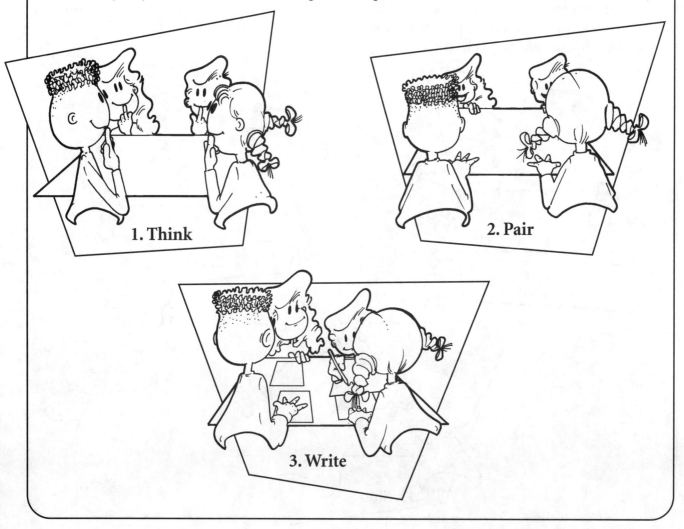

1. Think
2. Pair
3. Write

Virginia DeBolt: *Write! Science*

Cooperative Learning Structures

*Structure 24*

# Think-Write-Pair-Share

*In this variation of Think-Pair-Share, students write down their own ideas before they pair up to discuss them with a partner. Think-Write-Pair-Share allows students to more fully develop their own ideas before sharing them.*

After the think time, students write down their own ideas. This allows more reflective students and students who develop their thinking through writing explore the question or issue in more detail before they are asked to share their ideas with a partner. When students pair up, they read what they wrote to their partner, then discuss the issue more. The added writing component often leads to a richer pair discussion. Select a few students to share their writing, their partner's writing, or the ideas they discussed with the class.

1. Think
2. Write
3. Pair
4. Share

Virginia DeBolt: *Write! Science*

Cooperative Learning Structures

**Structure 25**

# Think-Write-RoundRobin

*After a question or topic is announced by the teacher, students "Think" about the question, "Write" down their ideas on the topic, then "RoundRobin" read their writing to teammates. Think-Write-RoundRobin allows students to develop their ideas on a topic, as well as hear the ideas of teammates.*

The teacher announces a question to the class. Students are given 10-15 seconds of think time, then are instructed to write down their ideas. After ample writing time, students RoundRobin read their writing to teammates.

1. Think

2. Write

3. RoundRobin

Virginia DeBolt: *Write! Science*
Kagan Cooperative Learning • 1 (800) WEE CO-OP

# Unstructured Sort

*Students work as a team to develop their own system for sorting items or information. Unstructured Sort develops classification, categorization and sorting skills.*

In Unstructured Sorts, students generate a number of ideas or copy a number of ideas on separate note cards. The cards are spread out so that everyone can see them. Teams are instructed to sort the items into two categories. To sort the items, students take turns placing each item in the category system. When done, students work together as a team to create a new categorization system. Then, students take turns again placing the items in their new categorization system.

In Team Sort students are given the categories and some type of categorization system such as a Venn diagram. In Unstructured Sorts, it is up to students to develop their own categorization systems.

Cooperative Learning Structures

Structure 27

# Write-Pair-Share

*After a question or topic is announced by the teacher, students "Write" down their ideas, "Pair" up with a partner to read what they wrote, then some students are selected to "Share" their ideas with the class. Write-Pair-Share allows students to develop their own ideas in writing before sharing with others.*

Write-Pair-Share is a simple variation of Think-Pair-Share. After the teacher announces the question or topic, students are instructed to write down their answer or ideas instead of just thinking about them. Writing helps many students more fully develop their ideas on the topic and enriches the subsequent pair discussion. When students are done writing or after a predetermined amount of writing time, students pair up and read what they wrote to their partner. Pairs can further discuss the question or topic after sharing each other's writing. As a final step, the teacher invites a few students to share what they or their partner wrote with the entire class.

1. Write

2. Pair

3. Share

Virginia DeBolt: *Write! Science*

# Bibliography

**Bloom, Benjamin S., et al.** *A Taxonomy of Educational Objectives: Handbook 1: Cognitive Domain.* Longman, New York, 1977.

**Campbell, Linda, et al.** *Teaching and Learning Through Multiple Intelligences.* New Horizons for Learning, Stanwood, WA, 1992.

**DeBolt, Virginia.** *Write! Cooperative Learning and the Writing Process.* Kagan Cooperative Learning, San Juan Capistrano, CA, 1994.

**Gere, Anne Ruggles, ed.** *Roots in the Sawdust: Writing to Learn across the Disciplines.* National Council of Teachers of English, Urbana, IL, 1985.

**Kagan, Laurie, Kagan, Miguel, and Kagan Spencer.** *Teambuilding.* Kagan Cooperative Learning, San Clemente, CA, 1997.

**Kagan, Miguel, Robertson, Laurie and Kagan, Spencer.** *Classbuilding.* Kagan Cooperative Learning, San Clemente, CA, 1995.

**Kagan, Spencer.** *Cooperative Learning.* Kagan Cooperative Learning, San Clemente, CA, 1994.

**Kagan, Spencer and Kagan, Miguel.** *Advanced Cooperative Learning: Playing with Elements.* Kagan Cooperative Learning, San Clemente, CA, 1994.

**Kagan, Spencer and Kagan, Miguel.** *Multiple Intelligences: Teaching With, For, and About MI.* Kagan Cooperative Learning, San Clemente, CA, 1998.

**Parks, Sandra and Howard Black.** *Organizing Thinking, Book 1.* Critical Thinking Press & Software, Pacific Grove, CA, 1992.

**Shaw, Vanstan and Kagan, Spencer.** *Communitybuilding.* Kagan Cooperative Learning, San Clemente, CA, 1992.

**Tompkins, Gale.** *Teaching Writing: Balancing Process and Product.* Macmillan, New York, 1994.

**Zinsser, William.** *On Writing Well: An Informal Guide to Writing Nonfiction.* Harper Perennial, New York, 1994.

# About the Author

Virginia DeBolt has been teaching for thirty years in Colorado, New Mexico and Texas. She is currently teaching English at Murchison Middle School in Austin, Texas. She has worked with all ages from kindergarten to adult, but enjoys most the opportunity to work with other teachers and share ideas about writing and cooperative learning. She is interested in publishing students' writing on the internet and is creating a web home page for her school. Her personal home page can be viewed at http://www.flash.net/~vdebolt.

## More Books by Virginia

### Write! Cooperative Learning and the Writing Process

Three methods to make your students better writers: Have them 1) Write! 2) Write! and 3) Write some more. You receive ready-to-use writing lessons in each of the writing domains: imaginative, functional, communication, non-fiction/reporting, and opinion making. Cooperative learning structures are used at each of the stages of the writing process: prewriting, writing, proofing and editing, conferring and rewriting, and publishing. Includes practical management tips, references, resources, and ideas for evaluating students' writing with portfolios, holistic scoring, primary trait scoring, analytic, self evaluation, and peer evaluation.

### Write! Across the Curriculum Book Series

Move beyond drill and kill. Teach for understanding. Integrate writing across the curriculum! When students write in science, social studies and mathematics, they delve deeply into content and issues, their thinking is clarified and they obtain a deeper understanding and appreciation for the content. Writing makes the content accessible to your verbal/linguistic students. Each book includes 36 multiple intelligences, cooperative writing activities with ready-to-use reproducible activity pages, and brief descriptions of dozens of strategies. Teammates work cooperatively on these writing activities. Writing activities are a perfect way to start the class, introduce a new concept, end the unit, or use as a sponge activity.

### Write! Mathematics
Includes activities like writing the steps of solving a problem, composing word problems, restating definitions, and translating the language of math

### Write! Science
Includes activities like keeping a science log, defining science concepts, writing how something works, prioritizing world problems, coming up with a new invention.

### Write! Social Studies
Includes activities like writing the correspondence of two historical characters, publishing and sharing political cartoons, discussing and writing about famous historical quotations.

*Available from Kagan Cooperative Learning*

# Professional Development!

**Kagan Cooperative Learning Proudly Offers Top-Notch Professional & Staff Development Opportunities...**

★ Consulting Services

★ Graduate Courses

★ MI National Tour

★ Summer Institutes

★ Workshops

## Bring  to Your School or District!

*We make it easy to set up the best in-service your school or district has ever experienced! Bring in a certified member of the dynamic Kagan consulting team for one of the following fantastic workshops:*

- Cooperative Learning Intro (Getting Started)
- Block Scheduling & Secondary Restructuring
- Creating the Cooperative School
- Hands-On Science
- Higher-Level Thinking
- Math with Manipulatives
- Multicultural Classroom
- Multiple Intelligences
- Peer Coaching for Teachers
- Primary Classroom
- Second Language Learning (ESL)
- Social Studies
- Strategies for Inclusion
- Teambuilding & Classbuilding
- Whole Language
- Writing Process

*Come learn how to boost achievement, prevent discipline problems, and make learning more fun and meaningful for you and your students!*

**Call for More Info!**

**1 (800) CO-OP LRN**
1 (800) 266-7576

**Or Visit Us Online!**
www.KaganCoopLearn.com